Endorsements

"Gates, bars, guards, razor wire, guns, and guard dogs surround the place where a man sits alone in a cell with more freedom in his soul than any lost man on the outside. Dr. Roy Bell, though behind man-made confinements became freer than he had ever been when Jesus Christ, the living Son of God, took up residence inside that prison in a man crying out to God in repentance and faith. The Lord Jesus Christ makes you FREE, even though locked behind physical bars."

– Kevin Mann, Editor of the *First Mention Study Bible*

"I have known Bro. Bell since he was released from prison. His is an amazing story of how GOD opens doors and GOD will greatly use a willing vessel. He has definitely proven himself willing and labored to be a vessel fit for the Master's use. His story is DEFINITELY worth reading with attention."

– Evangelist Cliff Taylor, Onesimus Ministries

"Brother Roy's testimony is an amazing picture of God's redemptive grace and a stunning picture of His promise to never leave or forsake His born again children. Give this book to anyone who needs assurance of their salvation or motivation to stay in the race. TO THE FIGHT!!!"

– Geoffrey Grider, Now the End Begins Ministries

"I first heard Bro. Roy's story in the mountains of North Carolina. I was captivated as he testified of God's ability to use a man surrendered to Him no matter the circumstances or location. God uses WHOM He chooses, WHERE He chooses. I am excited to see what God will continue to do with Bro. Roy and this work that he has authored."

– Randy Keener, Evangelist and Author

"I've worked as a chaplain in correctional services for 21 years and had the honor of supervising and being an eyewitness of the miraculous and progressive sanctification of Roy as I worked with him, and I can truly say that he's a living Lazarus and a testimony of what the Lord has and is and will continue to do."

– Chaplain Julio "Chap" Calderin

"Years ago, as a chapel worker in High Desert State Prison, Brother Roy reached out to us at Bible Baptist Church in Las Vegas to go minister to the men there. We did that with Roy for years and still go to the prison. Roy, however, was miraculously released from prison and now serves the Lord here at our church. How all that happened, you just have to read for yourself."

– Pastor Mitch Serviss, Bible Baptist Church in Las Vegas, NV.

Justified

Outlaw

My Testimony and Some Things I Learned Along the Way

Evangelist Roy Bell

SIMMONS SE7EN

PUBLISHING

JUSTIFIED OUTLAW

Copyright © 2024 Roy Bell

All Rights Reserved

SIMMONS SE7EN PUBLISHING

Akron, OH 44307

www.simmonsopinions.com

I would like to dedicate this book to many people that God has used in my life, but will limit it to three: Dr. Peter S. Ruckman, who taught me the Book.

Chaplain Julio "Chap" Calderin, who modeled what a minister is supposed to be.

And my daughter, Haley, who loved and forgave an old Outlaw who missed most of her life, and today is my best friend in the whole world.

Table of Contents

Section 1: Preface

    You Can't Run from God . . 13

Section 2: Voices

What is a Man?	51
The Conflict	59
The Enemy	73
The Cross	85
The Christian's Battle	95
Spirits of Fear	115
The Voice of God	125
Father and Master	135
Our Blessed Hope	145
The Attack on Grace	161
Counterfeits . .	171

Section 3: Prologue

    The Final Word . . . 191

Part 1: Preface

You Can't Run from God

I am Roy Bell from Las Vegas, Nevada and I am a member of Bible Baptist Church in Las Vegas. People want to hear my crazy story, you know? And to tell you the truth, I kind of get tired of telling it, right? I want to preach the word!

I don't want to talk about me, and people told me, "No, listen. God's using that and people are interested in it. So, you keep telling it."

Right now, I'm gonna attempt to give my testimony and I always start with a scripture. Philippians chapter 1 and verse 6 reads, **"being confident of this very thing, that he which hath begun a good work in you will perform it until the day of Jesus Christ."**

Okay, let me just say this right at the outset – the best testimony that anybody could have is to get saved at seven, backslide when you're eight, get right at nine, and live for Jesus the rest of your life. That's the ideal testimony.

My testimony is not ideal, but a lot of people have testimonies like mine. Justification and sanctification are two separate things. We're not saved by who we are and, what we do, and how good we are. You'll hear this a lot in religious circles and Calvinist or Arminian circles.

You know, somebody will get saved and everything, and folks around them will say, "we'll see. We'll see." That's damnable! That's damnable right there. You don't know! You don't know what's in his flesh and his past or what that person was dealing with. So, say the guy had an alcohol problem and he gets saved, and he goes along good for a month or so and there's those folks in the church saying, "yeah, we'll see if it was real."

A month or so goes by and he has a bad day, and he goes back and has a drink. Then that crowd's like, "yeah. I knew it." Yeah? Shame on us for even thinking like that, you know? That's kind of my story.

I grew up in Las Vegas. My dad was a casino boss who worked for Meyer Lansky and set up casinos all over the world. He was the "clean white guy without a record" that was the casino manager who ran things for "the fellas." That's what my dad did, but he died when I was 10 years old. I was in 14 different countries before I was 11 years old.

We were actually in Iran – this is when the Shah of Iran was in power. My dad was setting up a casino for the Shah, when my father had a massive heart attack. When we came back to Las Vegas, my mom had to go back to work and became a secretary at an elementary school.

You know how the story goes. I fell in with a rough crowd and by the time I was 15, I was getting locked up in juvenile prison for the first time.

I'd done every drug you could imagine and was burglarizing pharmacies around Las Vegas. I'm little now, but I was so tiny when I was in school that there was never even a girl smaller than me in all my years of school. They used to pat me on the head and say, "aren't you in the wrong school little boy?" and that was the kind of the beginning of the drugs and stuff.

I looked over at what we called back in our day, "the stoners," you know? I thought the stoners were cool and they were having a good time, and you know, they were the cool kids, and I was like, "man. I want to be one of those guys." So, I tried dope and, unfortunately, really liked it.

I've never done anything halfway. I dived head over heels. Just within a couple months of smoking my first joint, I'd tried every drug there was in every way there was to take it. I started burglarizing pharmacies. I mean, it just went that fast. So, I went three times through youth prison reform school.

I got out and, let me say at this point, that I grew up in a in a good home. My mom's a good person. My dad was a good person. I got a stepdad when I was 15. In 1975, my mom remarried a local dry cleaner in Las Vegas – a good man – but this was a Christless home.

My mom grew up Roman Catholic and just through seeing the hypocrisy and the phoniness of that system; she was a sharp lady, and she thought that none of that religion was real. As soon as she was old enough, she threw the baby out with the bath water and said, "I'm done. I don't want to hear any more that Jesus church stuff as long as I live," because of her experience growing up in the Roman Catholic Church. So, I never went to church a day in my life. I was never exposed to the Gospel a day in my life.

I was in the Las Vegas casino scene, and I did not even know that our church world here existed. When I would see stuff about it on tv, I just thought Jesus and the Bible were like Santa Claus and the Tooth Fairy. I mean like come on get out of here, you know? Forget about that stuff. That's not real. That's for little kids or something.

At 18, they kicked me out of reform school. When I turned 18, I kind of had the law on my tail and I went on a run. I went on the road, and I fell in with some outlaw bikers. I was down in Florida, Mississippi, and south Texas.

When it got to be around my 21st birthday, around December going right going into 1981, I was down there as far south as you could get in Texas on the Rio Grande River – south of Corpus Christi – at a place called Mission, TX. I was hanging out with the outlaw bikers, and we were running guns and dope across the river with other outlaw bikers and Mexican cartel drug dealers. I was getting ready to turn 21 years old, you know, and I can remember we had a little apartment there that we were working out of, and I remember sitting out on the porch one night and just looking up at the stars realizing I'm getting ready to turn 21.

I just felt like, "well, I guess my life is over. I'm on the run from the law. I'm a drug addict. This this where Roy Bell ends up. This is it for me, I guess." And I can remember kind of just looking out to the sky and the stars and thinking about if there was anybody out there, you know, for real.

Praise God there was somebody out there. There was somebody listening.

It was a very short time after that this the biker gang that I was hanging out with – the second generation of the Peacemakers from Toledo, OH that started right after World War II – and one of my friend's dads was one of the original founding members. I was in the second generation.

They started talking about one of the OG's – the original gangsters; the old guys – coming down. They started talking about big Dave Break coming down. Man, they talked about big Dave Break like he was Godzilla, Superman, Batman, James Bond, and King Kong all put together!

They started telling big Dave Break stories and how he went into the bar with a shotgun, kicked in the door and whooped 15 guys, took all their biker jackets, and ripped the patches off.

Well, what they didn't know was that big Dave got saved, and big Dave was now a biker for Christ!

We were going to see him, but he's specifically coming down there to his old people to share the Lord with them.

I remember the day that big Dave Break pulled up down there at the bottom of the stairs to that apartment on a Moto Guzzi 850 El Dorado. He came up the stairs and I knew the moment I looked at Dave Break, that whatever it was that this man had is what I've been looking for all my life. I just knew it and man, I'm dialed in on Dave and I'm gonna get this guy's number! I'm gonna figure this guy out, you know? We street wise guys peep somebody for a minute and we figure out what makes them tick pretty quick. That's how I'll find out what this guy's got!

He came into that apartment, and he sat down on the couch and began to talk about Jesus Christ, and I thought Jesus and the Bible were like Santa Claus and the Tooth Fairy. Within a moment of it, the Bible says, speaking of itself, **"For the word of God is quick, and powerful, and sharper than any twoedged sword, piercing even the dividing asunder of soul and spirit,**

and of the joints and the marrow, and as a discerner of the thoughts and intents of the heart. Neither is there any creature that is not manifest in his sight: but all things are naked and opened unto the eyes of him with whom we have to do" (Hebrews 4:12-13).

Dave said that the sword of the spirit is light, and these words are light, and these words are power. I can remember the very scripture that he quoted that pierced the darkness of my soul and let the light in.

He said, "I want to know Him and the power of his resurrection." I didn't know what it was just about that particular verse, but that thing came in like the Holy Spirit reached down there and flipped on a light switch. I was like, "what? Jesus and the Bible? Jesus is real. The Bible is true. Jesus and the bible. This is crazy."

This is real and I'll tell you, in that moment I was wonderfully, wonderfully saved and born again! The Lord came into me!

I didn't know any theology. I didn't know any certain salvation formula. All I knew is this guy said, "Jesus was the answer," and I could see Jesus all over him. I said "yes" to the Gospel. It opened my heart and Jesus came in my heart too. I was saved and I've been saved since that day. There was a little southern Baptist church there in Mission, TX and I started just walking there every day.

They didn't even have church services, but I can remember walking down to that little church every day. I'm talking about when the sun was shining and the birds were singing, I was walking this high off the ground, like I was floating. I got a dose of the Holy Ghost for sure, man!

I was so happy, and through a series of circumstances, I ended up going through that church at Lester Roloff's boys homes out of Corpus Christi, TX. They had a boy at one of those homes from the church, and he rescued one of the director's little boys who fell through the ice in a frozen pond. He got the little boy out, but he went back under and drowned. He was a boy named John Orcott, and he died there. They brought his body back to this church here to brother Bob Wills from the Roloff operation who was running the Redemption Ranch Boys Home right outside of Hattiesburg, Mississippi. They came down with four boys from the home to attend the funeral of John Orcott in this little church after I'd been saved a week.

I didn't know anything. You know? I didn't. I just knew Jesus and I now wanted to be where Jesus was. So, I'm in church and those boys got up and gave their testimony in that funeral service. I went up to Bob Wills after the service. I said, "can I go with you, Bobby?"

He looked at me and said, "well, what are you saying, Roy? You want to be a missionary?"

I said, "yeah, that's it! I want to be a missionary."

He said, "well, we're leaving in the morning," and I said, "I'll be ready!"

So, we loaded up and headed to Redemption Ranch. On the way, we stopped in Corpus Christi and saw brother Roloff. I slept on his living room floor that night. The next morning brother Roloff got up and fixed us breakfast. He looked at Bro. Wills and then looked at me.

"He said who is that?" asked Roloff.

Brother Wills said, "oh, that's brother Roy. He's gonna be a missionary."

I've been saved for a week, you know? And Bro. Roloff said, "go and get him a haircut, won't you? He don't look like one of our boys."

We went to the Redemption Ranch, and I moved to Hattiesburg where I started going to Bible college.

From there, I went to Hyles-Anderson College and fell in love with the most beautiful, and probably best Christian I ever met in my life. There was a girl there and she was in tune with God, but it wasn't time to get married. I thought it was, but she kind of broke my heart and I hadn't been saved very long, so I got mad at God.

I was at Hyles-Anderson College, and one of my dorm mates there – and there were eight of us in the dorms – said something snappy about her, so I busted his face all up. You don't do that in Bible college. In the meantime, I was talking to her and was like, "Kathy, I'll leave you alone. Look me in the eyes and tell me you don't love me."

And she goes, "I do, I do, but it's not time and my dad said I'm not supposed to date you." She continued, "well, I'm gonna go talk to my dad one more time."

She called, but meanwhile I beat up my roommate. She goes and calls her dad, and he calls the college and tells them, "I want this guy away from my daughter."

The next day, I was in the dean's office because I beat up my roommate and I'm "stalking" this girl. So, they kicked me out and I got bitter. I got mad at God. I said, "you know what? I got brainwashed or something." I tried to take it all back, and that's when my run from God started. I tried to take it all back, but you can't run from somebody that lives inside of you. He's there to stay.

The Bible says, **"But he that is joined unto the Lord is one spirit"** (1 Cor. 6:17). You can't run from yourself because you and He are one. I tell you, if anybody ever gave God a good run for the money, it was me. So, I went back to Las Vegas and that started my run; my Jonah journey.

I was called and was even being trained for the ministry when I tried to take it back. I said, "no I'm gonna go back," like when Jonah went down to Tarshish. He went down into the ship, down into the whale's belly, and he went down into hell. Well, he went down four times, and I went down four times. I had four separate prison terms and ended up spending 30 years of my life in the penitentiary, but that wasn't the length of my sentence.

I was sentenced to like 100 or something years, but I ended up spending 30 calendar years in the penitentiary – not even counting boys homes and reform school. There were a few times during that period where I kind of half-hearted tried to get right a little bit, but the drugs would come back into my life, and I'd fail.

Then some of that crowd would go, "see! Told you so! He ain't saved, you know! There's no way he could be saved! He gets saved then goes to prison? He wasn't saved. You know that."

But I was!

I just kept struggling with the dope. I got off dope for a couple years there in 1992-96. I got out and my stepdad had a dry-cleaning business in Vegas. I was working in the family business, and I married one of my counter girls. We had a daughter. I bought a home. I mean everything was rosy! But I fell back on the dope, and I went back to prison again.

These last two prison terms were each 12 years and there were only 10 months between the two 12-year terms so that was really long stretch. On this last one, I was 50 years old and got strung out on dope again. I had a Harley XL 1200 Sportster, and I started going out pulling licks, you know, doing robberies, around Vegas on my Harley. They called me "The Motorcycle Bandit," because they got after me a couple times and I shook them. Then, on the last robbery, the helicopter spotted me on the freeway. I led them on a 45-minute chase all around Las Vegas with a helicopter and 40 ground units, but they finally got me and slammed me on the hood of the cop car when they finally put the cuffs on.

I was 50 years old at that point, and I said "yeah, I'm dying in prison now for sure. No, ifs ands or buts

about it." Then I went to court. What did they give me? A 10 to life. They gave me a life sentence at age 50!

Now, a 10 to life means you will see a parole board in 10 years. But listen, when you've got 12 felony convictions, you've escaped from prison twice, and have two habitual criminal enhancements, you don't make your parole board with a record like that. They just say, "we'll see you again in five years."

You come back in five years. Yeah, we'll see you in another five years. We call it "wear you out." They're wearing you out on one of those, right? So, there was no way in the world I was ever going to make up my first board on that.

While I was in prison, finally, I was like, "okay. Well, I'm done now. I'm done. I'm going to spend the rest of my life in prison." I accepted that fact and that is when I finally tapped out and I said, "okay. Listen. If I'm going to be in prison for the rest of my life, at least I want my joy back. I want my peace back. I'm going to do it with the Lord and if I'm going to be here for the rest of my life, I'm done chasing the dope." And God, even at that point in time, took the desire from me.

I'll show you what else He did. They tested me when I got to prison. I shot a lot of dope in my life, and they tested me when I got there. They found I had antibodies to hepatitis c. So, they put me on the hep c chronic care program. During that time, they came out with the treatment and the pill where they could cure it.

So, I said, "okay. I want the treatment. Cure me!" and they say, "no. We're only going to administer the treatment if your liver starts to fail. We're just going to monitor you. You're hep c positive, but we're going to monitor you until your liver starts failing. Then we'll come cure you."

And so, I said, "no," and started a grievance; a lawsuit to try to make them give me that treatment. I still have the Inmate Grievance Report asking them to please cure me right now. I also have the official response that says the following:

> Inmate Roy Bell, I'm in receipt of your grievance #20063107512 as it relates to your request for hepatitis c treatment. According to your chart you had a follow-up with the provider on September 10th, 2020, for hepatitis c chronic care. Per doc, HC quantitative detects negative hepatitis RNA. You were exposed but didn't contract hepatitis c. Physicians orders – Discontinue from hepatitis c chronic care. Grievance resolved.

They say it's something like one in a million that clears the virus naturally, and I know that God did that when I when He delivered me from wanting to do dope; from the desire – the liking even for dope. He also healed my body of what the dope had done to me because I didn't know it yet, but He had a future for me, and a hope in the future. So, I got right with God. I had not been going to church. I hadn't been going to chapel because I got tired of making God look bad. I got tired of disappointing people every time I went back and restarted. I'd mean well, but then I'd fall off again and disappoint people and look like a hypocrite.

I thought, man, I'm just not going to do that anymore. I knew I was saved – in the midst of it all I never doubted my salvation. I knew I was saved, but this was just my thorn in the flesh. This is what I'll struggle with for the rest of my life. This is just me, Lord.

So, this all happened and the whole dope thing just went away. And the Lord's like "well, what's holding you up now? You're not gonna go back in the dope."

I'm like, "no." And He said, "well, then go to chapel."

So, I went to chapel and sat in the back. Now, I thought that the ministry ship had long sailed. I thought preaching was over with; it was way in the past, but they kind of recognized me like sitting way in the back. They were like, "brother Roy, would you open us up in a word of prayer?"

I couldn't hide it, and long story short, within a very short amount of time, I was assigned to the chapel as the chaplain's assistant. It was a 4,000-man prison, and each unit had its own chapel day. Monday through Friday, each unit would come down for Christian services. During the last decade that I was in prison, my job was to get up from my cell, go down to the chapel, and have church every day.

Back in 1990, in prison, I started writing Dr. Peter Ruckman and he started writing me back. He was my friend, my pen pal, and my mentor for 25 years. He sent me every book he ever wrote. I mean, he just had great influence in my life. So, everything I had learned through all that time and everything now that I know was what I was teaching in that chapel all week every week all those years.

I was "pastor Roy" and "brother Roy" all that time on the yard, and yet I knew I was going to die in prison. I just knew that, but I was in the center of God's will doing what He called me to do. I earned my doctorate in theology from Bible Baptist College of America and Southern Indiana Baptist College while I was incarcerated at High Desert State Prison.

During that time my daughter, whose whole life I missed, was really disappointed. She was mad at me, and there was a point in time where she was like, "I don't think I'll ever talk to him again." She had my first grandchild and that kind of put her in a more family minded thing.

One day when they were feeding us, they brought mail in and the officers up in the unit got to sort all this mail out. One of them got the clipboard out, finds the inmate, locates the cell, and writes it on the list. Then they have to sort it all and bring it to us. It's a lot of work, right?

Well, the guy was bringing the mail bag in one night and didn't want to do that work. He stopped by the dumpster next to the unit and dumped all our mail in the trash then came back in. But then the guys were feeding in the morning went out to dump the breakfast trash in the dumpster and saw the letters in there. So, it was like full stop. They turned over the dumpster, pulled everything out, and had a whole crew of guys wiping off letters.

Oh, that officer got in serious trouble, but about two days later – and my daughter hadn't talked to me since I missed her life and got locked up – but two days later an old, dirty, wiped off, wet letter came to my cell. I opened it up and it was from my daughter, Haley. It said, "Dad, I just want to let you know that I love you and I forgive you and I want to rebuild our relationship."

That's when it started. That's when she just had my first grandchild, and now I have two grandchildren. And, to this day right now, she and I are best friends. Best friends, best friends, best friends. I mean, we're like we're like two little girls, taking pictures of what we're eating and texting. There might be people that are as close to their daughter as I am to mine, but there ain't nobody closer to their daughter than I am to mine. God completely rebuilt that thing!

Now, I didn't get the wife back, but, you know, that's not on her. That's on me. I was supposed to never get out of prison, so she moved on. But she's a good friend and even comes to church with us. My daughter comes to church with us too. My grandkids come to church with us. Everybody's still there in church. It's all good. God put that thing together.

While I was in prison, before I ever even knew I was going to get out, I saw on tv – I never had a cell phone. I never had a computer, and I didn't know anything about this stuff – but on my little tv there in the cell I saw the birth of the whole phenomenon and YouTube. And I was like, "man, if I ever got out, I'd get on and have one of them YouTube channels."

My daughter helped me set up that YouTube channel, but I knew what it was going to look like. God gave me the vision of it, and I drew it years before I ever did get out. I drew it and if you guys have ever watched my YouTube channel, you'll see that come to life. There's a little Charlie Brown looking Roy Bell in his little suit, and behind him is his little bookshelf and his little jacket. God brought that to pass.

Now, my YouTube channel, Old School Bible Baptist, has nearly 21,000 subscribers and I've made over 700 videos. I linked that up with Facebook and posted all my stuff over on Facebook, and that's where I met certain people. So, God's just blessed that.

I've been able to preach well over a hundred times in about 30 churches in probably 20 states. These last three years have just been an absolutely amazing whirlwind of God's blessing that I never, never, never, never imagined. I mean, flying into SeaTac (Seattle-Tacoma) Airport, picking up a rental car, staying in the Hilton — whoever thought that was going to happen, brother?

I've pinched myself sometimes, you know? But life is good, and God is good. He doesn't work on our timetables. He doesn't judge as a man judges. He is the great physician and as that verse says, He will finish that good work He started in you. And what it's going to take to finish that work in you is different than what it's going to take to finish that work in me.

He is the great physician, and He knows how to prescribe what we need. He's never going to prescribe too little medication that won't do the job, and He's never going to put too much on you that you don't need either. It's always going to be just right, and I just thank Him for just the honor and the privilege.

He took me by the scruff of the neck, and He opened up a big old steel cell and threw me in there. He took a King James Bible and chucked it in there after me. He said, "you learn that Book like you're supposed to, and you get your heart right so you can do something with it and maybe, just maybe, one day I'll come open that door."

I had perfect peace and joy. I did not feel like a prisoner. I felt like a missionary that just lived on the field and I said I'm going to be here the rest of my life, and I was completely good with that. Then Covid hit.

What happened when Covid hit was that people quit going to work. Do you know what happens to a prison when the employees of the prison quit coming to work? The place fails. It completely fails. The prison was locked up. They slammed our cell doors and did not open them again for two years. We did not have exercise, sunshine, fresh air, yard time; nothing. They came around about every three days, handcuffed you, took you for a five minute shower, and put you back in the box. That's what we did for two years.

The state of Nevada was just like, "we got to do something. People are still out there committing crimes and coming to prison, but we have got nobody to watch them. We've got nobody to feed them." So, they decided that anybody that's eligible for parole that hasn't killed somebody was going to be let go May 3, 2021.

They let me go on my first parole board on that 10 to life. If it hadn't been for Covid, I would never have walked out of there. They let me out on May 3rd. That was three years this last May.

Thirty years in a cell went by, then I heard a jingle, jingle, jingle in the hallway. They were coming with the keys and that door opened, and the Lord said, "well, ol' Roy. You ain't got much time left. You want to come out and go to work for a little while?"

I said "yes," and on May 3, 2021, I got out of prison.

I am 𝔍𝔲𝔰𝔱𝔦𝔣𝔦𝔢𝔡 𝔒𝔲𝔱𝔩𝔞𝔴.

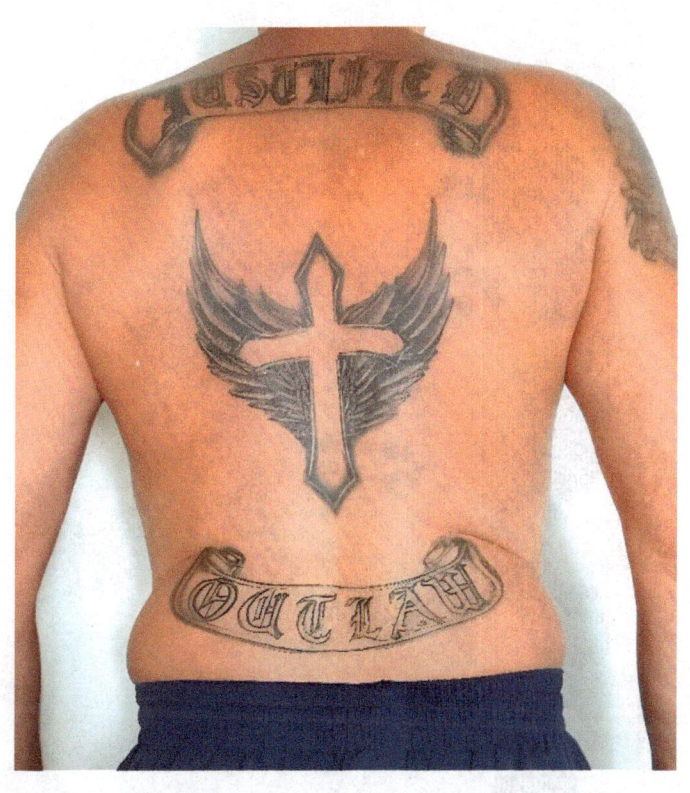

JUSTIFIED OUTLAW - 35 -

JUSTIFIED OUTLAW - 37 -

Off-duty trooper aids in carjack arrest

Karen Zekan
Fri, May 15, 1998 (2:28 a.m.)

An off-duty Nevada Highway Patrol trooper who witnessed a bank robbery suspect carjack a senior citizen Thursday resorted to gunfire to slow the thief's getaway car before Metro Police could take him into custody.

Roy Burney Bell, 38, an ex-felon for robbery and burglary, was in handcuffs shortly before 6 p.m. after attempting to run from the intersection of Eastern Avenue and Russell Road where he rammed the hot car into another vehicle, Metro Lt. Wayne Petersen said.

The off-duty trooper who initiated the apprehension had been shopping in the Von's grocery store at 3325 E. Russell Road about 5:30 p.m. when he witnessed a man with a bandana over his face and guns in either hand approach a teller at the Bank of America branch inside the store, Petersen said.

As the suspect fled with a bank bag filled with cash, the trooper followed, arming himself with his off-duty weapon, police said.

The suspect then robbed a senior citizen at gunpoint, taking the elderly person's car and speeding out of the parking lot.

"As the suspect was driving away, the NHP trooper identified himself verbally," Petersen said. "The suspect pointed his weapon at the trooper as he was driving away. The trooper, fearing for the safety of citizens in the area ... (fired) two rounds in a downward direction at the tires of the vehicle in an attempt to disable it and prevent the suspect from escaping."

The trooper's rounds missed the tires, but responding Metro officers took up the chase and made the eventual capture. Police recovered the money and the suspect's weapons.

Local briefs

Tue, Aug 31, 1999 (10:51 a.m.)

Sentencing set in prison break

District Judge Jeffrey Sobel has set Oct. 12 for sentencing of inmate Roy B. Bell, who escaped from the Southern Desert Correctional Center in Indian Springs by hiding in the undercarriage of a delivery truck in January.

Bell, who pleaded guilty to one felony count Monday in District Court, was arrested several days after his escape in Las Vegas after a pizza restaurant was robbed.

The Department of Prisons beefed up its security at Indian Springs after the Bell escape, Attorney General Frankie Sue Del Papa said.

JUSTIFIED OUTLAW- 39 -

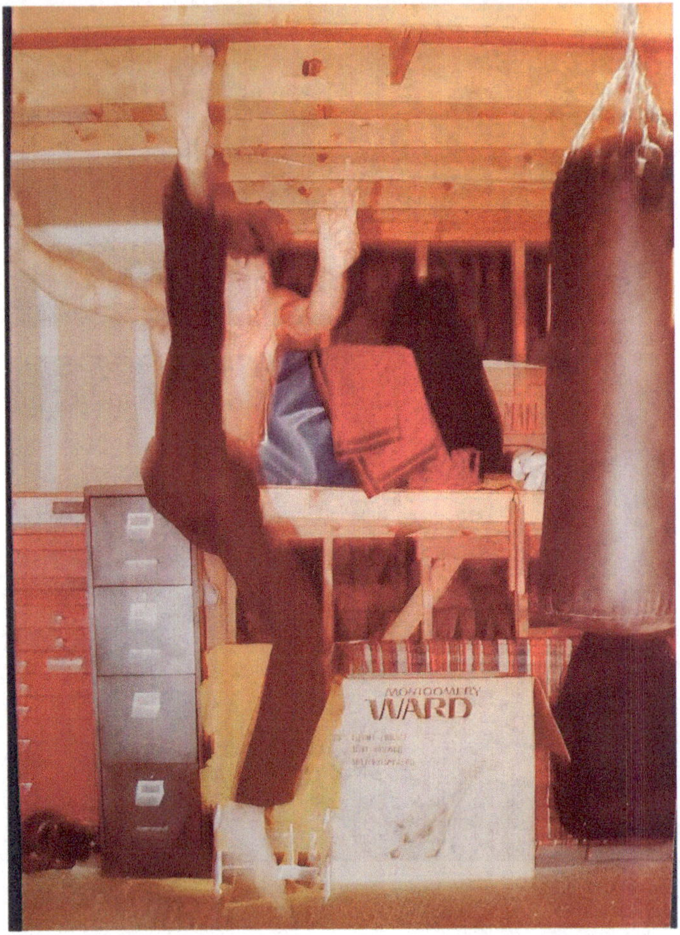
MONTGOMERY
WARD

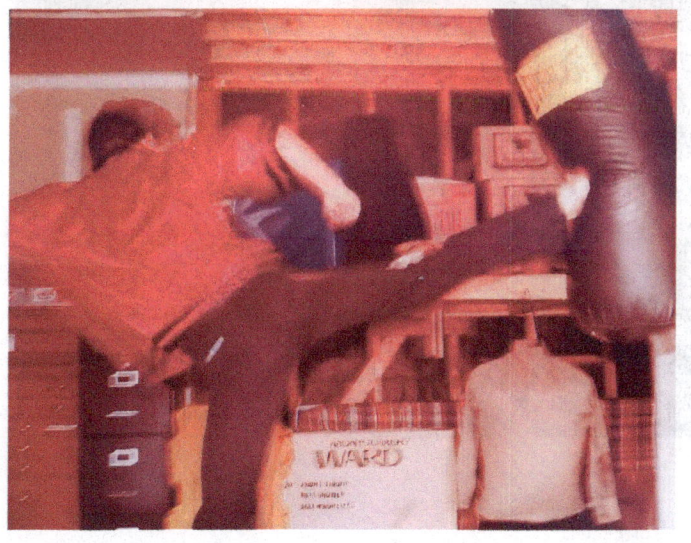

JUSTIFIED OUTLAW - 41 -

High Desert State Prison

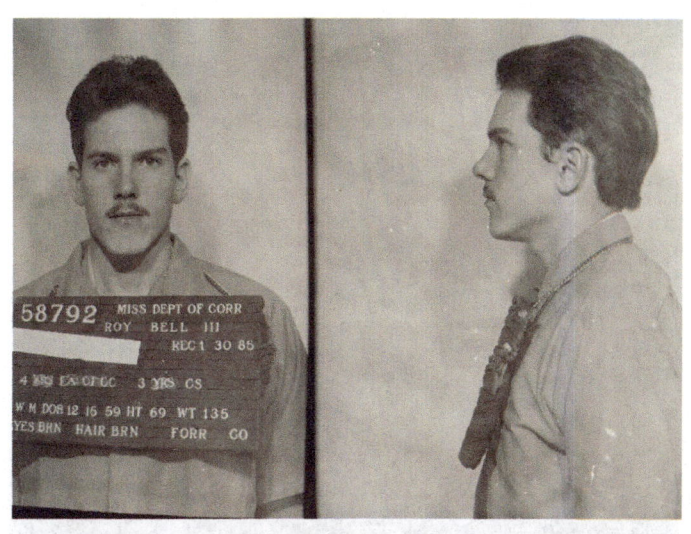

JUSTIFIED OUTLAW

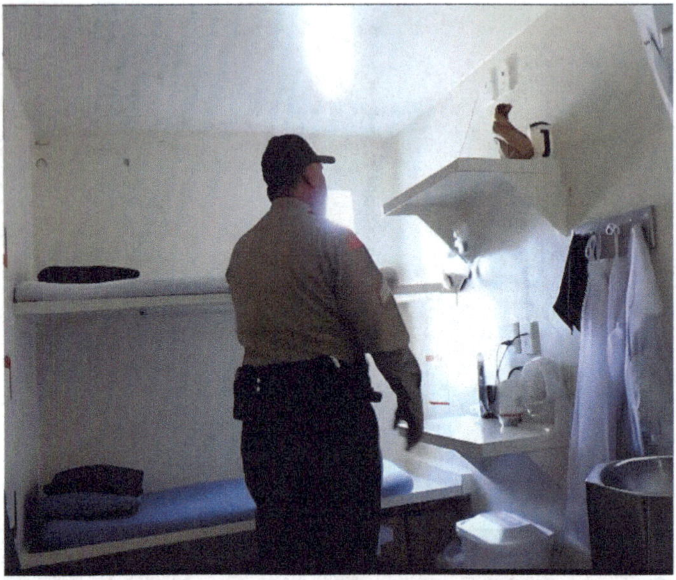

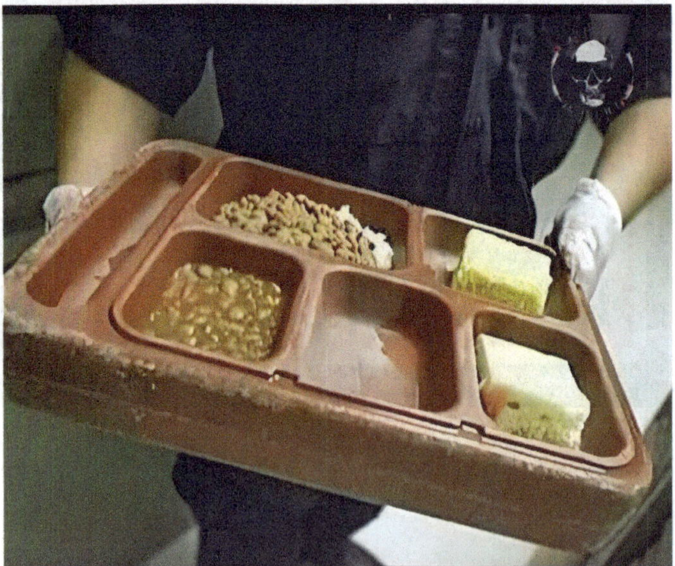

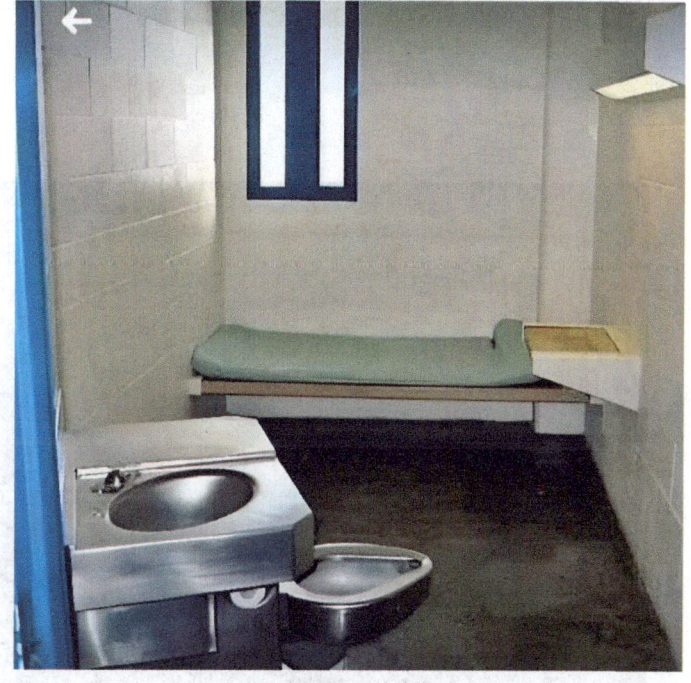

JUSTIFIED OUTLAW

Identification and Demographics

Name	Offender ID	Gender	Ethnic	Age	Height	Weight	Build	Complexion	Hair	Eyes	Institution	Custody Level	Aliases	Prior Felonies
ROY B BELL	26514	Male	CAUCASIAN	62	5'8"	150lb	MEDIUM	FAIR	BROWN	BROWN	PAROLE	LOW/SSIGNED	ROY BLONDY BELL	YES

Booking Information

Offense Code	Offense Description	Sent. Status	Sent. Min	Sent. Max	Sent. PED	Sent. MPR	Sent. County	Sent. PED	Sent. Type	Sent. XBD	Sent. Start Date
350B	HABITUAL CRIMINAL (LESSER)	Discharge to Consecutive		0 yr. 144 mo. 0 days	2002-05-18		CLARK COUNTY COURTHOUSE	1990-05-05	DETERMINATE		1988-12-27
193	ROBBERY	Discharge to Consecutive	0 yr. 24 mo. 0 days	0 yr. 60 mo. 0 days	2050-09-05		CLARK COUNTY COURTHOUSE	2002-02-31	DETERMINATE		1938-09-07
193	ROBBERY, LBW	Discharged	0 yr. 24 mo. 0 days	0 yr. 60 mo. 0 days	2000-04-05		CLARK COUNTY COURTHOUSE	2002-02-31	DETERMINATE		1938-09-07
193S	USE OF DEADLY WEAPON ENHANCEMENT	Discharge to Consecutive	0 yr. 24 mo. 0 days	5 yr. 60 mo. 0 days	2000-04-18		CLARK COUNTY COURTHOUSE	2005-04-09	DETERMINATE		2003-06-01
140R	VICTIM OVER 65 ENHANCEMENT	Discharged	0 yr. 24 mo. 0 days	0 yr. 60 mo. 0 days	2002-03-31		CLARK COUNTY COURTHOUSE	2005-04-09	DETERMINATE		2002-06-01
193	ROBBERY	Discharged	0 yr. 35 mo. 0 days	0 yr. 120 mo. 0 days	2009-05-18		CLARK COUNTY COURTHOUSE	2011-05-05	DETERMINATE		2005-05-15
403	ESCAPE	Discharge to Consecutive	0 yr. 19 mo. 0 days	0 yr. 120 mo. 0 days	2007-04-18		CLARK COUNTY COURTHOUSE	2011-05-03	DETERMINATE		2003-06-15
347A	HABITUAL CRIMINAL (GREATER)	Parolee	10 yr. 0 mo. 0 days		2011-05-03		CLARK COUNTY COURTHOUSE		LIFE WITH PAROLE		20 05-04

Inmate Photo

Parole Hearing Details

Offender Book ID	Parole Hearing Date	Parole Hearing Location
7362	1991-05-13	SOUTHERN DESERT CORRECTIONAL CENTER
7362	1994-05-14	SOUTHERN DESERT CORRECTIONAL CENTER
7362	1998-05-14	SOUTHERN DESERT CORRECTIONAL CENTER
7362	1999-04-07	SOUTHERN DESERT CORRECTIONAL CENTER
7362	2001-06-21	ELY STATE PRISON
7362	2006-04-19	ELY STATE PRISON
7362	2008-07-11	PAROLE BOARD ROOM 101
7362	2009-02-26	PAROLE BOARD ROOM 201
7362	2010-07-15	HIGH DESERT STATE PRISON
7362	2021-05-27	PAROLE BOARD ROOM 301

Southern Indiana Baptist College

Upon Recommendation of the Faculty we have hereby conferred upon

Roy Bell

after satisfactorily completing the prescribed requirements for the degree of

Doctor of Theology

with all the honors, rights, and privileges appertaining thereto
here and elsewhere
In Witness Whereof, the authorized officers are hereunto
Given this Sixth day of February, Two thousand twenty.

It is appointed unto men once to die, but after this the judgment
For the wages of sin is DEATH
but the gift of God is ETERNAL LIFE
There is a way that seemeth right unto a man, but the end thereof are the ways of death.
Believe on the Lord Jesus Christ, and thou shalt be saved
I'M GOING TO LET GOD FIX IT BECAUSE IF I FIX IT I'M GOING TO JAIL

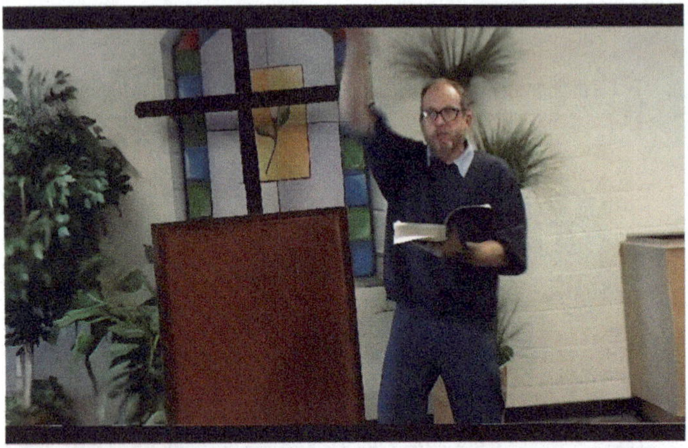

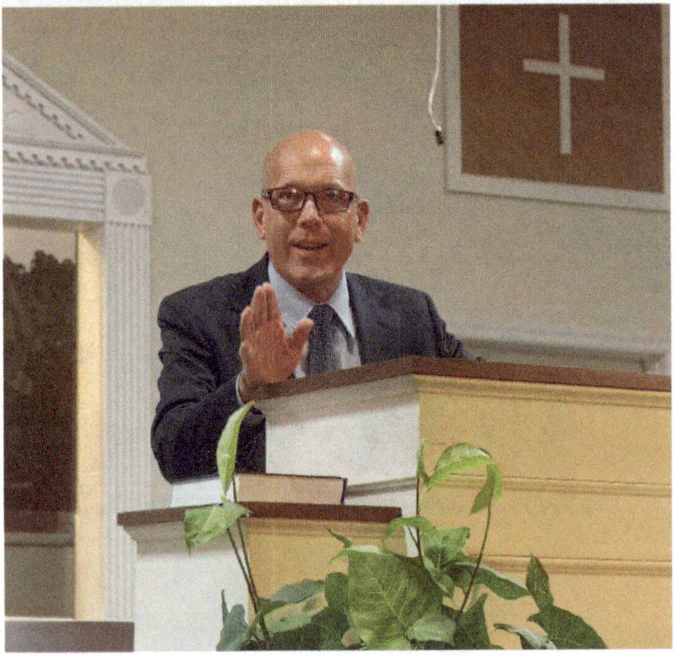

Part 2: Voices

Chapter One – What is a Man?

For we wrestle not against flesh and blood, but against principalities, against powers, against the rulers of the darkness of this world, against spiritual wickedness in high places

Ephesians 6:12

The Apostle Paul here says there is behind the material world perceived by our senses, a spiritual world inhabited by spiritual beings. Paul's premise is that regardless of how it is manifested in the material world, the first cause of thought and subsequent behavior finds its origin in the spiritual realm.

The apostle says that there is a battle being waged 24 hours a day, 365 days a year for the heart and mind of each and every one of us. The purpose of this book is to bring to light what may be known about this conflict. We will be examining human thought.

I'm not a doctor of psychiatry. How the brain works chemically, and manifests thought and emotion, I will leave to those with expertise in that area. Medical science and the various theories and speculations of psychiatric medicine will not be our subject.

Our focus will be the first cause, or the genesis, of the thoughts that the brain processes. This study will pierce through the physical material veil of the flesh and discover a world and reality that secular academia knows nothing about. We will be talking about spiritual things.

We will not engage in speculation, but we'll deal with the sure and certain authority of revelation. I make absolutely no apology whatsoever to anyone for trusting the 66 books of the Holy Bible as the inspired and perfectly preserved words of the one true and living God. That Book is, therefore, our Final Authority on all matters material or spiritual.

The very fact that this truth has been hidden from the minds of most people is evidence of the existence of an enemy and his cover-up campaign. Listen to what the Apostle Paul has to say about that, **"But if our gospel be hid, it is hid to them that are lost: In whom the god of this world hath blinded the minds of them which believe not, lest the light of the glorious gospel of Christ, who is the image of God, should shine unto them"** (2 Corinthians 4:3-4).

Most people are in complete spiritual darkness and unable to perceive spiritual truth. Paul describes that spiritual condition in 1 Corinthians 2:14, **"But the natural man receiveth not the things of the Spirit of God: for they are foolishness unto him: neither can he know them, because they are spiritually discerned."**

What Paul is saying is that a person in their natural state perceives only the physical material world. They are unable to receive spiritual light and truth. Why is that? It is because we are broken inside.

How are we broken inside? To answer that question, we would first have to answer the question, what exactly is a man? Sad to say, secular academia, modern medical science, the political and social leaders of the world, all of them, regardless of the degrees, titles, or accolades behind their names, have one thing in common. They cannot tell you exactly what a man is. You must go to the source.

You have to go to the words of the one who made man before we talk about the spiritual world's impact and influence on man. We must define exactly what a man is, as must happen in your spirit first to fix what is broken before light can get in. Volumes and volumes have been written proving the Bible to be the Word of God.

I'm not going to do that here. I'm simply going to pull the trigger. God's words have a power all their own.

What is a man? **"And God said, let us make man in our image and our likeness"** (Genesis 1:26).

God said He made us in His image. So, what is the image of God? Paul tells us, **"For the invisible things of him from the creation of the world are clearly seen, being understood by the things that are made,**

even his eternal power and Godhead; so that they are without excuse" (Romans 1:20).

Paul says here that if we will look at what God made and we will see His image, or Godhead, revealed in His creation. What is the Godhead? The Apostle John tells us, **"For there are three that bear record in heaven, the Father, the Word, and the Holy Ghost: and these three are one"** (1 John 5:7).

This is where the term "Trinity" comes from. Tri means three. Unity means one. Trinity simply means these three are one. Paul said that if we look at what God made, we will see the Trinity. So, what did God make? Well, first of all, He made the universe.

The universe consists of three elements. Reality itself is three-dimensional and consists of time, space and matter. Time isn't space. Space isn't matter. Matter isn't time, but they are one thing – the universe.

Time is past, present, and future. Space is height, width, and depth. Matter is liquid, solid, and gas.

The elements of each of these are absolutely distinct one from another but make up one inseparable thing. An atom is electron, neutron, and proton. On earth, you have animals, vegetables, and minerals. You have land, sea, and air.

Light has three kinds of rays: Those you can see but not feel, those you can feel but not see, and those you cannot see or feel. The examples go on and on.

When God made man in his own image, this is how He did it: **"And the Lord God formed man of the dust of the ground, and breathed into his nostrils the breath of life; and man became a living soul"** (Genesis 2:7).

He made a body and formed man of the dust of the ground. He breathed his spirit into man, breathed into his nostrils the breath of life, and man became a living soul.

Paul says, **"I pray God your whole spirit and soul and body be preserved blameless . . ."** (1 Thessalonians 5:23).

Man is a trinity too – three distinct elements that make one man. He is three-in-one. If I may borrow an illustration from one of my mentors, think of a man like a football. The pigskin is the body, the inner tube is the soul, and the air inside is the spirit.

The body is the seat of your physical senses. It is world conscious. The soul is the spiritual body – the seat of the mind, will, and emotions, and is self-conscious. Your soul is the same shape as and looks like you. It is your ghost and is part of you that will exist somewhere for all eternity.

You are not your body; you are inside of your body. You may have heard the expression the eyes are the windows to the soul.

The word spirit comes from the same word as wind or air. Jesus said, **"God is a Spirit: and they that worship him must worship him in spirit and in truth"** (John 4:24). The spirit in man is God conscious.

The spirit is where a person is related to and perceives God. The spirit is the part of man required to receive spiritual light and truth. If the spirit is dead or broken, light and truth cannot be received.

Spiritual light and truth require a healthy receptive organ, just like it requires eyes to see color and ears to hear sound in the Garden of Eden. Before man fell into sin, God ruled the spirit. The spirit ruled the soul. The soul ruled the flesh. Man walked with God.

There was only one rule and one possible sin. Genesis 2:17 says, **"But of the tree of the knowledge of good and evil, thou shalt not eat of it: for in the day that thou eatest thereof thou shalt surely die."**

Did Adam's body die the day he and Eve ate the fruit? No. Adam was 930 years old when his body died.

Adam and Eve died spiritually the moment they ate of the fruit. They were spiritually separated from God and, had God not made provision for the salvation of their souls, would have experienced everlasting death. **"For as in Adam all die, even so in Christ shall all be made alive"** (1 Corinthians 15:22). Mankind coming out of the garden is broken inside, and we are born broken.

We are born wrong. Our spirit is dead. We are devoid of spiritual life.

We are a flat football. What a person needs is an infusion of spirit from outside of himself to bring his broken spirit back to life and restore his relationship to God. God made that possible by his work at the cross.

Having taken sin out of the way by paying for it Himself, it is now possible for a holy God to once again take up residence inside a man's spirit and for that spirit to be born again. This is what is meant by being a born again Christian. Our spirit is born again by the Holy Spirit, who is God, and He takes up residence inside of us.

He instantly imparts eternal life to our souls even as He begins the lifelong process of making us into the image of God. This person can receive spiritual light and truth because they have eyes to see again. That breaks mankind down into two categories – born once in Adam and dead in sin or born again in Christ and reconciled to God.

When we speak of the natural man, unregenerate man, or lost sinners, we are referring to those whose spirit have not been born again. When man died spiritually, the soul ceased to be ruled by the spirit.

By default, the soul began to run the show for the purpose of pleasing the self and feeding the desires of the flesh. Paul, talking to born again believers about their prior condition, says unto them, **"And you hath he quickened, who were dead in trespasses and sins; Wherein in time past ye walked according to the course of this world, according to the prince of the power of the air, the spirit that now worketh in the children of disobedience: Among whom also we all had our conversation in times past in the lusts of our flesh, fulfilling the desires of the flesh and of the mind; and were by nature the children of wrath, even as others"** (Ephesians 2:1-3).

Spiritually dead people are being controlled in thought and behavior by external spiritual entities. But don't think for a moment that the born-again Christian is not also under constant attack and influence of these same spiritual forces.

Who or what are they? Where did they come from? What powers do they have? How do they work? Most importantly, how are they defeated? Are you interested? Read on.

Chapter Two – The Conflict

And there was war in heaven: Michael and his angels fought against the dragon; and the dragon fought and his angels

Revelation 12:7

We human beings are newcomers on the stage of the universe and are part of an ancient conflict which God has allowed in order to glorify Himself and share His love and glory perfectly with His creation, **"And to make all men see what is the fellowship of the mystery, which from the beginning of the world hath been hid in God, who created all things by Jesus Christ: To the intent that now unto the principalities and powers in heavenly places might be known by the church the manifold wisdom of God, "According to the eternal purpose which he purposed in Christ Jesus our Lord"** (Ephesians 3:9-11).

God or the YHWH, the eternal self-existent one, the I AM, is a spirit. He exists outside of his construct called time. For the benefit of those in His created universe who are in time, He is allowing a grand drama to be played out in the universe. Planet Earth being center stage in this conflict. Genesis 1:1 states, **"In the beginning God created the heaven and the earth."** God later asked Job, **"Where wast thou when I laid the foundations of the earth? declare, if thou hast understanding . . . When the morning stars sang**

together, and all the sons of God shouted for joy?" (Job 38:4, 7). These were and are the created sons of God – the angelic host.

The prophet Ezekiel tells us that there was a manifestation of the throne of God on earth in the garden of Eden at that time, and that the greatest of all created beings, Lucifer, was the anointed cherub over God's throne.

In all descriptive visions of the throne of God – Ezekiel 1, Isaiah 6, and Revelation 4, we see four living creatures around the throne called cherubim or seraphim. There used to be five. Look how Ezekiel describes the garden of Eden and God's throne there before Lucifer's fall, and the description of his fall. A lot of Bible commentators totally missed this in Ezekiel 28:12-18:

> **Son of man, take up a lamentation upon the king of Tyrus, and say unto him, Thus saith the Lord God; Thou sealest up the sum, full of wisdom, and perfect in beauty. Thou hast been in Eden the garden of God; every precious stone was thy covering, the sardius, topaz, and the diamond, the beryl, the onyx, and the jasper, the sapphire, the emerald, and the carbuncle, and gold: the workmanship of thy tabrets and of thy pipes was**

prepared in thee in the day that thou wast created. Thou art the anointed cherub that covereth; and I have set thee so: thou wast upon the holy mountain of God; thou hast walked up and down in the midst of the stones of fire. Thou wast perfect in thy ways from the day that thou wast created, till iniquity was found in thee. By the multitude of thy merchandise they have filled the midst of thee with violence, and thou hast sinned: therefore I will cast thee as profane out of the mountain of God: and I will destroy thee, O covering cherub, from the midst of the stones of fire. Thine heart was lifted up because of thy beauty, thou hast corrupted thy wisdom by reason of thy brightness: I will cast thee to the ground, I will lay thee before kings, that they may behold thee. Thou hast defiled thy sanctuaries by the multitude of thine iniquities, by the iniquity of thy traffick; therefore will I bring forth a fire from the midst of thee, it shall devour thee, and I

> **will bring thee to ashes upon the earth in the sight of all them that behold thee.**

This is the holy mountain of God on earth in Eden. The description of the covering sounds a lot like New Jerusalem that comes down to earth in eternity.

The history of the universe starts and ends with the throne of God manifest on earth. Everything in between is what we call Bible study. That throne and kingdom is the theme of the Bible.

Lucifer is the fifth cherubim that covers the throne here in Eden. He sins because of his beauty. He is accused of merchandise and traffic as the anointed cherub that covereth.

He would have been like a high priest over the worship of God. The cherubim cry, "holy, holy, holy." Lucifer began to believe that his beauty and glory were an inseparable part of himself and came from him.

He began to take a cut, if you will, and skim the glory of God for himself. Isaiah 14:12-14 describes this:

> **How art thou fallen from heaven, O Lucifer, son of the morning! how art thou cut down to the ground, which didst weaken the nations! For thou hast said in thine heart, I will ascend**

into heaven, I will exalt my throne above the stars of God: I will sit also upon the mount of the congregation, in the sides of the north: I will ascend above the heights of the clouds; I will be like the most High.

Lucifer sought not only to be independent of his creator, but to replace Him. This is Lucifer's rebellion. The Bible tells us that one-third of the angels followed him in his rebellion in Revelation 12:3-4. The Bible talks about the dragon and his angels in Revelation 12:7, and reveals everlasting fire prepared for the devil and his angels in Matthew 25:41. These angelic beings or beings of some kind populated the earth.

In the Bible, angels are not disembodied spirits. They don't have wings. They appear as men with bodies.

Paul says all flesh is not the same flesh and that there are celestial bodies and bodies terrestrial in 1 Corinthians 15:40. These created sons of God, angelic beings, take human wives and have a half breed offspring, according to Genesis 6:2-4. These beings rebelled against God with Lucifer and were judged on earth with him. This occurs during the gap between Genesis 1:1 and Genesis 1:2. **"In the beginning, God created the heaven and the earth."**

Stop there. There's your gap. **"And the earth was without form and void and darkness was upon the**

face of the deep." Verse 2 describes the condition of the earth after God's judgment of Lucifer and his followers.

This is described in Psalms 82:1, 5, and 7, **"God standeth in the congregation of the mighty; he judgeth among the gods. They know not, neither will they understand; they walk on in darkness: all the foundations of the earth are out of course. But ye shall die like men, and fall like one of the princes."**

Job 9:5-7 describes the earth in a condition like we find it in Genesis 1:2, **"Which removeth the mountains, and they know not: which overturneth them in his anger. Which shaketh the earth out of her place, and the pillars thereof tremble. Which commandeth the sun, and it riseth not; and sealeth up the stars."**

Speaking about the great tribulation before his second coming, Jesus says, **"For then shall be great tribulation, such as was not since the beginning of the world to this time, no, nor ever shall be"** (Matthew 24:21). Jesus likens the great tribulation to something that happened at the beginning of the world.

Jeremiah does much the same thing in describing Christ's second coming in chapter 4, verses 23-16, **"I beheld the earth, and, lo, it was without form, and void; and the heavens, and they had no light. I**

beheld the mountains, and, lo, they trembled, and all the hills moved lightly. I beheld, and, lo, there was no man, and all the birds of the heavens were fled. I beheld, and, lo, the fruitful place was a wilderness, and all the cities thereof were broken down at the presence of the Lord, and by his fierce anger."

This gives us a description of what an earth that is "without form and void" looks like. It's wonderful how the Bible defines and interprets its own terminology. Amen.

Though not necessary to understand the scripture, the Hebrew text is interesting at this point. Without form and void in the Hebrew text are "tohu" for *without form* and "bohu" for *void*. Those are Strong's concordance numbers H8414 and H922 respectively.

They are defined as "tohu" – to lie waste, a desolation and a worthless thing and vain. And "bohu" is an indistinguishable ruin. Now look at this verse in Isaiah. It says, **"For thus saith the Lord that created the heavens; God himself that formed the earth and made it; he hath established it, he created it not in vain, he formed it to be inhabited"** (Isaiah 45:18).

The Hebrew word translated "in vain" here is tohu – the same word translated as "without form" in Genesis 1:2. So, God did not create the earth without form and void. Something happened in the gap between Genesis 1:1 and Genesis 1:2. When the text said "and the earth was," the word *was* can carry the same meaning as the word *became*.

Just as if I were to say, "after working all day I was tired," I could have said, "after working all day I became tired." They would carry the same meaning. As a matter of fact, the Hebrew text is interesting here as well.

The Hebrew word translated *was* in Genesis 1:2 is "haya" (Strong's H1961). It is the same word translated *became* in Genesis 19:26 where Lot's wife "became a pillar of salt."

God destroyed the earth and its inhabitants who followed Lucifer in his rebellion.

Lucifer is transformed into Satan, the Devil, although he can still appear as an angel of light (2 Corinthians 11:14). Satan's true form now is that of a reptile – **"And he laid hold on the dragon, that old serpent, which is the Devil, and Satan . . ."** (Revelation 20:2).

It is in that form that he appears to Eve in the renewed garden in which God told Adam to **"Be fruitful, and multiply, and replenish the earth"** (Genesis 1:28). That's the same thing he told Noah and his sons, **"Be fruitful, and multiply, and replenish the earth"** (Genesis 9:1).

You can't replenish the earth unless there was somebody there before. God says of the pre-Adamic inhabitants of the earth, **"they have filled the midst of thee with violence"** (Ezekiel 28:16).

Satan was transformed into a serpent; a dragon. His followers may have been as well, but we saw in Psalm 82 that they died like men. These angelic beings that the Bible calls the "sons of God," or "little g" gods, become disembodied spirits. These are what the Bible calls unclean spirits or devils.

If they were transformed into dragons before their destruction to reflect their violent nature, might there not be a layer of the earth's crust containing the remains of many large reptiles? Sometimes it's right there in front of you, my friend!

I am deeply indebted to the great Bible teachers of the last 150 years from whom I have learned so much. In 1876, G. H. Pember, in his book *Earth's Earliest Ages*, wrote:

> For may not these demons be the spirits of those who trod this earth in the flesh before the ruin described in the second verse of Genesis and who at the time of that great destruction were disembodied by God and left still under the power and ultimately to share the fate of the leader in whose sin they acquiesced? Certainly, one oft-recorded fact seems to confirm such a

theory, for we read that demons are continually seizing upon the bodies of men and endeavoring to use them as their own.

In 1911, Clarence Larkin, in his groundbreaking book *Dispensational Truth*, agrees the demons are not to be classed as angels. They appear to be disembodied spirits.

Some think of the pre-Adamite earth, the inhabitants being disembodied because of the sin that caused the pre-Adamite earth to become chaotic. This is plausible because they seek to re-embody themselves as human beings. They are wicked, unclean, vicious, and have the power to derange both mind and body.

They are the familiar spirits of the Old Testament and the seducing spirits of which Paul warned Timothy. Watchman Nee, the great Chinese pastor, evangelist, and martyr, also agrees. Teaching in the 1950s and recorded in the book, *The Mystery of Creation*, he says, "from the New Testament we can trace two orders of Satan's subjects, the angels and the demons."

Let us look at the angels first. **"Depart from me, you cursed, into eternal fire, which is prepared for the devil and his angels. In his, the dragon's, tale draweth the third part of the stars of heaven"**

(Matthew 25:41). The stars here refer to the angels. Cross-reference this with Revelation 1:20.

Revelation 12 continues later with these words, **"And the great dragon was cast out, that old serpent, called the Devil, and Satan, which deceiveth the whole world: he was cast out into the earth, and his angels were cast out with him"** (verse 9). These angels must be those spirits whom God had set in the beginning to assist the archangel to rule the world, rule the world. They are the "little g" gods in Psalms 82:1. Cross-reference this with John 10:35.

At the fall of Lucifer, these probably conspired with him, or at least they were in sympathy with him, and so they fell into sin with Satan and have now become the **"principalities," "powers," "the rulers of the darkness of this world," and "spiritual wickedness in high places"** (Ephesians 6:12). Satan has another order of subjects. These are evil spirits or demons.

Those demons or spirits probably were a pre-Adamic race who inhabited the former world. They either assisted Satan in rebellion or else they followed him afterwards, and thus they were destroyed by God by being disembodied. These beings have consequently become disembodied spirits.

As you can see, there are some different ideas about some of the details that there is no question about their existence. There exists all around us a spiritual world that is just as real in the material world that we can see. C.S. Lewis in his book *Mere Christianity* in 1943 says:

> But as soon as you look at any real Christian writings, you find that they are talking about something quite different from this popular religion. They say that Christ is the Son of God (whatever that means). They say that those who give Him their confidence can also become Sons of God (whatever that means). They say that His death saved us from our sins (whatever that means).
>
> There is no good complaining that these statements are difficult. Christianity claims to be telling us about another world, about something behind the world we can touch and hear and see. You may think the claim false; but if it were true, what it tells us would be bound to be difficult – at least as difficult as modern Physics, and for the same reason.

In his book, Clarence Larkin also says, "the scriptures are full of the supernatural. The only cure for the materialism of this present day is to discover what the scriptures reveal as to the spirit world. The dividing veil is our fleshly bodies."

He is so right.

Even back in 1911, there's something about being in this fleshly body that veils the spirit world from us. The instances in scripture where God pulled back the veil and gave people visions into the spirit world are numerous.

This is one of my favorites:

> **And when the servant of the man of God was risen early, and gone forth, behold, an host compassed the city both with horses and chariots. And his servant said unto him, Alas, my master! how shall we do? And he answered, Fear not: for they that be with us are more than they that be with them. And Elisha prayed, and said, Lord, I pray thee, open his eyes, that he may see. And the Lord opened the eyes of the young man; and he saw: and, behold, the mountain was full of horses and chariots of fire round about Elisha** (2 Kings 6:15-17).

In the spirit world around us, all the time, there are angels of God and demonic spirits of one order or another. All throughout Christ's ministry on earth, He spoke to and cast out demonic spirits, as did the apostles.

This is reality. **"For we wrestle not against flesh and blood, but against principalities, against powers, against the rulers of the darkness of this world, against spiritual wickedness in high places"** (Ephesians 6:12).

"Now the Spirit speaketh expressly, that in the latter times some shall depart from the faith, giving heed to seducing spirits, and doctrines of devils" (1 Timothy 4:1).

These spirits came to steal, kill, and destroy. They are minions of the adversary. There is a spiritual war, and their number one objective is to keep people from coming to know the Lord Jesus Christ as Savior and Lord.

"But if our gospel be hid, it is hid to them that are lost: In whom the god of this world hath blinded the minds of them which believe not, lest the light of the glorious gospel of Christ, who is the image of God, should shine unto them" (2 Corinthians 4:3-4).

Satan and his minions' number two objective is to keep those who do know Christ from walking in the power of the Holy Spirit; anything to keep the light of Christ from shining through you. That is the conflict you are engaged in today. How are you doing in the battle?

Chapter Three – The Enemy

And you hath he quickened, who were dead in trespasses and sins; Wherein in time past ye walked according to the course of this world, according to the prince of the power of the air, the spirit that now worketh in the children of disobedience

Ephesians 2:1-2

The prince of the power of the air; the god of this world. What can the Bible tell us about these powers or spirits of the air? Quite a lot, actually. The main type or similitude that the Bible gives for demonic spirits is birds. That is not surprising when we consider that Satan tries to counterfeit most everything God does.

When Jesus is baptized, we read, **"And the Holy Ghost descended in a bodily shape like a dove upon him"** (Luke 3:22). In the Parable of the Sower, Jesus identifies **"the fowls of the air"** who **"taketh away the word that was sown in their hearts"** (Mark 4:4, 15), as Satan and the wicked one (Matthew 13, Mark 4, and Luke 8).

Solomon says, **"Curse not the king, no not in thy thought; and curse not the rich in thy bedchamber: for a bird of the air shall carry the voice, and that which hath wings shall tell the matter"** (Ecclesiastes 10:20).

Look at Mystery Babylon in Revelation 18:2, **"And he cried mightily with a strong voice, saying, Babylon the great is fallen, is fallen, and is become the habitation of devils, and the hold of every foul spirit, and a cage of every unclean and hateful bird."**

So demonic spirits are like birds, and they fly around us in the air, all around us, all the time.

In fact, one of the Satan's names is Beelzebub, and it is used of him seven times in the Bible. Matthew 12:24 identifies him as "the prince of devils." Strong's Concordance defines Beelzebub as "Dung god, a name of Satan," in the Greek. It is number G954, and says it's a parody on the Hebrew Chaldee, number H1176, "Baal of the Fly," from H2070, Zebub, meaning "to flit a fly, especially one of a stinging nature."

Satan is lord of the flies. His minions are disembodied spirits. These devils are like flies in the atmosphere around us in the spiritual realm.

They are attempting to manifest Satan's will to such a degree as God allows. Like flies, they would have to be small. When Jesus confronts the demon-possessed man at Gadara, He asks the unclean spirit its name, and the reply is, **"My name is Legion: for we are many"** (Mark 5:9).

A Roman legion consisted of around 6,000 men. Six thousand fit in one man's body. Luke 8:2 says that

Mary Magdalene had seven devils cast out of her. They are small, but they are real, and they are busy.

Through them, Satan controls this world. He controls what people think and what they believe. All of the government, science, and education are under their control, as is most religious thought.

Their presence can be identified by the one universal consistent that runs through their message: None of this is real. We do not exist.

To fully understand how the spirits of the air are able to affect human thought and behavior, we must return to the internal makeup of a human being. Man, made in the image of God, is a trinity. In his original state, man's spirit was in the image of God's Spirit. It was sinless. With sin came death, and man's spirit died. **"Wherefore, as by one man sin entered into the world, and death by sin; and so death passed upon all men, for that all have sinned"** (Romans 5:12).

What is left is a soul joined to a body of death; cut off from the life of God. What the body does defiles the soul, and the defiled will of the soul manifests in the sinful acts of the body. Demonic spirits can speak into and even take up residence in the fallen spirit of a man.

They can and do possess these people at the deepest core of their being, their spirit. This is how all lost people are controlled by Satan, **"Wherein in time past** ye walked according to the course of this world, according to the prince of the power of the air, the spirit that now worketh in the children of disobedience"** (Ephesians 2:2).

An unsaved person has no defense. They are ultimately controlled by the devil.

Notice in the next verse that there are **"desires of the flesh and of the mind; and were by nature the children of wrath, even as others."** This is because the soul and the flesh are joined, or married, and feed off each other in the unsaved person. Manifestations of our fallen sinful nature are not only of the baser fleshly sort but run deeper into our will. This is our will acting independently of our Creator.

These run the course of **"vain imaginations"** (Romans 1:21) and their **"inventions"** (Psalms 106:29), which might not even appear to be evil or sinful but find their origin in a worldview that excludes the light of God's revelation of Himself. Paul warned Timothy of these in 1 Timothy 6:20, **"O Timothy, keep that which is committed to thy trust, avoiding profane and vain babblings, and oppositions of science falsely so called."**

Jesus told the religious and social leaders of that time, **"Ye are of your father the devil, and the lusts of your father ye will do. He was a murderer from the beginning, and abode not in the truth, because there**

is no truth in him. When he speaketh a lie, he speaketh of his own: for he is a liar, and the father of it" (John 8:44). This is true of every unsaved person, science, education, philosophy, and religion.

Any worldview that denies the biblical revelation of the gospel of the grace of our Lord and Savior, Jesus Christ, is a demonic worldview. It is a lie that will damn people to hell. Those who spread the lies are guilty of murder; co-conspirators in the damnation of a soul into **"everlasting fire, prepared for the devil and his angels"** (Matthew 25:41).

Just as Jesus said, **"the words that I speak unto you, they are spirit, and they are life"** in John 6:63. The words of Satan are death and hell, and he is the father of that too. When Satan and his followers rejected God, God gave them their wish and prepared a place for them.

These eternal beings must exist somewhere forever, and as they had rejected God's presence, God prepared a place without His manifested presence for them. God is omnipresent. It is impossible to be anywhere that God is not, but God prepared a place where His presence would not be perceived, so if all that is good comes from God, and He removes His presence, what does that leave?

Because God is light, this is a place of darkness. Since God is love, this is a place of hate. Since God is peace, this is a place of fear. Since God is joy, this is a place of sorrow. Since God is pleasure, this is a place of pain, and because God is hope, this place that Jesus said was eternal fire is a place of eternal doom. It is the only place an angelic being or the eternal soul of a man can exist who has rejected God and all that He is. Anyone who goes there chooses it of their own free will by rejecting God's revelation of Himself in Jesus Christ.

This is either a place of literal fire or something so much worse that there are no words in human language to describe it. The destiny of Satan and his angels is fixed. This is their place.

They sinned in full knowledge and absolute light while beholding the face of God. When God was manifest in the flesh, **"he took not on him the nature of angels; but he took on him the seed of Abraham,"** according to Hebrews 2:16.

"Forasmuch then as the children are partakers of flesh and blood, he also himself likewise took part of the same; that through death he might destroy him that had the power of death, that is, the devil" (Hebrews 2:14).

"And almost all things are by the law purged with blood; and without shedding of blood is no remission" (Hebrews 9:22). The God-man, Jesus

Christ, shed His blood and reconciles man back to God. There was no bloodshed for the fallen angels.

There is no redemption for them, and they know it. That is the one reason they hate us so much, but they hate God more. Their only way of getting back at Him is to take as many of us as they can with them to that place prepared for them.

The sad news is most people will choose Satan. Jesus tells us why, **"And this is the condemnation, that light is come into the world, and men loved darkness rather than light, because their deeds were evil. For every one that doeth evil hateth the light, neither cometh to the light, lest his deeds should be reproved"** (John 3:19-20).

And this is just heartbreaking. **"Enter ye in at the strait gate: for wide is the gate, and broad is the way, that leadeth to destruction, and many there be which go in thereat: Because strait is the gate, and narrow is the way, which leadeth unto life, and few there be that find it"** (Matthew 7:13-14).

That is why Isaiah 5:14 says, **"Therefore hell hath enlarged herself, and opened her mouth without measure: and their glory, and their multitude, and their pomp, and he that rejoiceth, shall descend into it."**

The way is narrow, but it is there for whosoever will. **"Jesus saith unto him, I am the way, the truth, and**

the life: no man cometh unto the Father, but by me" (John 14:6). Everything Satan does is for the purpose of keeping people from finding the way.

Dr. Donald Gray Barnhouse, in his expositions on the book of Romans, said, "Our world, our whole world is an illusion created by Satan to deceive us, and the only spiritual truth in life is to be found in the word of God. Those who refuse the word are unable to see, because they have rejected light, have adopted other standards which they think are light, and are therefore in greater darkness."

Talk about a conspiracy theory! Everything we've been told all our lives is a bunch of lies from the devil. Everything from the imagination to invention has been diabolically designed to present a reality that excludes God's revelation of Himself. Science, education, philosophy, religion, news, entertainment, music, etc. all present a world without the God of the Bible. They want a place without Him. They have it in the form of this present evil world.

That is why John says, **"Love not the world, neither the things that are in the world. If any man love the world, the love of the Father is not in him"** (1 John 2:15).

And James said in chapter 4 verse 4 of his book, **"Ye adulterers and adulteresses, know ye not that the friendship of the world is enmity with God?**

whosoever therefore will be a friend of the world is the enemy of God."

Satan is essentially a religious being. His fall was a direct result of his desire to receive the worship that belongs only to God. He told Christ in the wilderness, **"All these things will I give thee, if thou wilt fall down and worship me"** (Matthew 4:9).

His grand hour will come during the end-time tribulation period, where he will be manifested in the flesh in the Antichrist. **"And all that dwell upon the earth shall worship him, whose names are not written in the book of life of the Lamb slain from the foundation of the world"** (Revelation 13:8).

Throughout history, Satan and his angels have sought out and received the worship of men. Paul told the Corinthians, **"But I say, that the things which the Gentiles sacrifice, they sacrifice to devils, and not to God"** (1 Corinthians 10:20).

"For though there be that are called gods, whether in heaven or in earth, (as there be gods many, and lords many,)" (1 Corinthians 8:5). This was man's predicament throughout human history. He was under the power of Satan, the god of this world and all his "little g" gods.

Individual men did find grace with God during these times, and we will talk about that later. But men were, for the most part, ignorant of the one true God of the Bible. Today is no different.

"Now the Spirit speaketh expressly, that in the latter times some shall depart from the faith, giving heed to seducing spirits, and doctrines of devils; Speaking lies in hypocrisy; having their conscience seared with a hot iron" (1 Timothy 4:1-2).

"Having a form of godliness, but denying the power thereof: from such turn away. Ever learning, and never able to come to the knowledge of the truth" (2 Timothy 3:5, 7).

Satan and his angels are as busy in the religious world as they are anywhere, maybe more so. Remember, his greatest desire is that men not find the way he has roadblocks and detours beyond number to shortstop every seeker. Thus, you have your multitude of world religions, large and small, old and new.

You have you have had, since the first century, sects that name the name of Christ, but do not offer the Christ or the Gospel of the Bible. We call them non-Christian cults. Then you have Christian denominations who actually believe in Christ and the Gospel but are so laden down with doctrinal errors and man-made traditions that they have made themselves of no effect.

Much of Christianity today has so compromised with this world and its ways that you can't tell the difference anymore, and they have become of no effect.

Chapter Four – The Cross

And we know that we are of God, and the whole world lieth in wickedness. And we know that the Son of God is come, and hath given us an understanding, that we may know him that is true, and we are in him that is true, even in his Son Jesus Christ. This is the true God, and eternal life

1 John 5:19-20

The whole world lies in wickedness under the god of this world, Satan.

Those who belong to him and share his destiny are the spiritually dead. They are flat footballs – live body, live soul, dead spirit. Because the Son of God has come and given us an understanding, we know Him, and we know that we are in Him.

"We have passed from death unto life" (John 5:24). How does that work? Something brand new came into being with the finished work of Jesus Christ on Calvary's cross. Everything changed.

Understanding that is the key to understanding the Bible. Before Jesus paid for sin on the cross, no one's soul could go to heaven when they died. Those souls still had sin on them and could not go into God's presence.

Before the cross, in the heart of the earth, there were two waiting rooms: one for the righteous dead and one for the wicked dead. The righteous dead were waiting for sin to be paid for so that they could go to heaven. They were comforted in a place called paradise, or Abraham's bosom.

The wicked dead are waiting in hell for the day of judgment when they will be cast into the lake of fire with the Devil and his angels. During the Old Testament times, the righteous dead were those who walked in the light they had. Paul laid that all out in Romans 2:7-8, **"To them who by patient continuance in well doing seek for glory and honour and immortality, eternal life: But unto them that are contentious, and do not obey the truth, but obey unrighteousness, indignation and wrath."**

How was that manifested? **"For when the Gentiles, which have not the law, do by nature the things contained in the law, these, having not the law, are a law unto themselves: Which shew the work of the law written in their hearts, their conscience also bearing witness, and their thoughts the mean while accusing or else excusing one another;)"** (Romans 2:14-15).

People in the Old Testament times were saved by grace through faith, but their faith was demonstrated, or made complete, by works. It was a faith plus works program.

They believed God and acted upon what He had shown them. Those who believed God and lived their lives in hope of his future reward. When they died their souls went to paradise where they continued to wait in hope for the manifestation of God's grace and their eternal reward. They had to wait until sin was taken out of the way. **"And for this cause he is the mediator of the new testament, that by means of death, for the redemption of the transgressions that were under the first testament, they which are called might receive the promise of eternal inheritance"** (Hebrew 9:15).

"The Holy Ghost this signifying, that the way into the holiest of all was not yet made manifest" (Hebrews 9:8). Once Christ paid for sin on the cross, sin was taken out of the way and the veil of the temple – the way into the holiest of all – was ripped wide open for those prisoners of hope.

This is what Isaiah prophesied 750 years before it happened, **"Thus saith the Lord, In an acceptable time have I heard thee, and in a day of salvation have I helped thee: and I will preserve thee, and give thee for a covenant of the people, to establish the earth, to cause to inherit the desolate heritages; That thou mayest say to the prisoners, Go forth; to them that are in darkness, Shew yourselves"** (Isaiah 49:8-9).

Paul looks back on the same event in Ephesians 4:8-9, **"Wherefore he saith, When he ascended up on high,**

he led captivity captive, and gave gifts unto men. (Now that he ascended, what is it but that he also descended first into the lower parts of the earth? He that descended is the same also that ascended up far above all heavens, that he might fill all things)."

What is Jesus talking about? **"[S]o shall the Son of man be three days and three nights in the heart of the earth"** (Matthew 12:40).

This is why His burial is one of the three parts of the gospel: The death, burial, and resurrection. When Jesus died on the cross, His spirit went back into heaven (Luke 23:46).

His body was placed in the tomb, but His soul descended into the lower parts of the earth. **"[H]e went and preached unto the spirits in prison"** (1 Peter 3:19). He preached condemnation to those in hell.

He then crossed the great gulf separating paradise from hell and entered paradise. He preached the good news of deliverance to those prisoners of hope and took them all to heaven with Him, transferring paradise to the third heavens (2 Corinthians 12:2, 4). That changed everything.

Oswald Chambers said, "there is nothing more certain in time or eternity than what Jesus Christ did on the cross. The cross is the center of time and eternity.'

Now, if you're a born again child of God, when you leave this body at death you are instantly with Christ in heaven.

"We are confident, I say, and willing rather to be absent from the body, and to be present with the Lord" (2 Corinthians 5:8). Why is that? It is because of the amazing thing that happens to a person when they receive Christ and are born again.

This is New Testament salvation – a brand new thing. Nothing like it ever happened to anybody before the cross. Most Christians do not know the details of this operation of God, much like someone who takes their car to the shop to have it repaired. Ask them exactly what the mechanic did under the hood, and they don't know. All they know is that the car works again. What God did under your hood is a blessing and important to understand.

What happens when a person gets saved? Paul puts it like this, **"In whom ye also trusted, after that ye heard the word of truth, the gospel of your salvation: in whom also after that ye believed, ye were sealed with that holy Spirit of promise, Which is the earnest of our inheritance until the redemption of the purchased possession, unto the praise of his glory"** (Ephesians 1:13-14).

So, a person hears the gospel, trusts and believes on Christ, and is then sealed by the Holy Spirit. Salvation was paid for by Christ, faith is the link that acquires it, and the Holy Spirit applies it – **"Ye must be born again"** (John 3:7). That is the Holy Spirit's job. This is a brand new thing.

Colossians 1:26-27 says, **"Even the mystery which hath been hid from ages and from generations, but now is made manifest to his saints: To whom God would make known what is the riches of the glory of this mystery among the Gentiles; which is Christ in you, the hope of glory."**

The Holy Spirit makes us one with God by his presence in us. Jesus said, **"for he dwelleth with you, and shall be in you . . . and my Father will love him, and we will come unto him, and make our abode with him"** (John 14:17, 23).

Paul said, **"Know ye not that ye are the temple of God, and that the Spirit of God dwelleth in you?"** (1 Corinthians 3:16). Because sin has been taken out of the way a holy God can now indwell a person and become one with them, as Paul again tells us, **"But he that is joined unto the Lord is one spirit"** (1 Corinthians 6:17).

And if it isn't enough that the Creator of the universe has taken up residence inside of us, He has also placed us inside of Himself – **"for by one spirit are we all baptized into one body"** (1 Corinthians 12:13), and **"For as the body is one, and hath many members,**

and all the members of that one body, being many, are one body: so also is Christ" (verse 12).

Since our spirit is one with His spirit, we are in Him. Every born-again believer since the cross is part of a new spiritual organism, the Body of Christ – the universal, invisible Church – **"for his body's sake, which is the church"** (Colossians 1:24).

Because we are spiritually in Him, He **"hath raised us up together, and made us sit together in heavenly places in Christ Jesus"** (Ephesians 2:6).

"[H}e is the head of the body, the church" (Colossians 1:18). Because we are part of His body, and He is resurrected and seated in heaven, our spirits have also been resurrected. Our spirits are just waiting for our souls and bodies to catch up. That is **"the earnest of our inheritance until the redemption of the purchased possession"** in Ephesians 1:14.

That means that it is paid in full; guaranteed. Now, let's look at how the Holy Spirit did that. Let's take that look under the hood. When the Holy Spirit took up residence in you, He performed a surgical procedure on you. Paul explains it in Colossians 2:11-12, **"In whom also ye are circumcised with the circumcision made without hands, in putting off the body of the sins of the flesh by the circumcision of Christ . . . the operation of God."**

Paul says that your soul is loosed from your fleshly body because **"our old man is crucified with him, that the body of sin might be destroyed"** (Romans 6:6).

That body of sins of the flesh is dead and can be cut off, or circumcised. That is made possible because **"ye are become dead to the law by the body of Christ; that ye should be married to another, even to him who is raised from the dead"** (Romans 7:4).

Before salvation, the soul is joined to the body. They are one flesh – married. Christ's death on the cross did away with your body of flesh, so now your soul can become one with, or marry, Jesus Christ. You are **"now members of his body, of his flesh, and of his bones. This is a great mystery: but I speak concerning Christ and the church"** (Ephesians 5:30, 32), and this is the result.

"I am crucified with Christ: nevertheless I live; yet not I, but Christ liveth in me: and the life which I now live in the flesh I live by the faith of the Son of God, who loved me, and gave himself for me" (Galatians 2:20).

This operation is what ensures your eternal security, because your sins can no longer defile your soul. It has been cut loose from the body and sealed by the Holy Spirit. When a believer's soul leaves his body at death, it is instantly in heaven, where his spirit already is. That is why we can claim with 100% certainty that a born again child of God is once saved always saved. We will discuss how God deals with sin in the believer's life in a later chapter.

What God does this does in this wonderful operation is take a sinful man out of this sinful world and make him holy, then puts him back into that sinful world and keeps him holy again. This is New Testament salvation. There's never been anything like it before the cross. Salvation and eternal rewards were a package deal received after death both dependent on faith and works.

For us today, in Christ, we receive salvation now by faith without works and our eternal rewards after death are based on our works. The cross changed everything. Of the times before the cross, Paul says that God **"in times past suffered all nations to walk in their own ways"** (Acts 14:16). He goes on to say, **"And the times of this ignorance God winked at; but now commandeth all men every where to repent: Because he hath appointed a day, in the which he will judge the world in righteousness by that man whom he hath ordained; whereof he hath given assurance unto all men, in that he hath raised him from the dead"** (Acts 17:30-31).

Peter also makes this very clear, **"Neither is there salvation in any other: for there is none other name under heaven given among men, whereby we must be saved"** (Acts 4:12).

This is the message of salvation for this day and age – the Church age; the age of grace – since the cross. This is the only way for a sinful man to be reconciled to a holy God. **"And, having made peace through the blood of his cross, by him to reconcile all things unto himself; by him, I say, whether they be things in earth, or things in heaven"** (Colossians 1:20).

This is the light and truth that Satan and his minions fight against. The unsaved are under their dominion but still possess a will, for that is what the soul is – the seat of the mind, the will, and the emotions. If you didn't have a will, you wouldn't have a soul. It is not the mind but the will that the Holy Spirit targets in the lost. When that heart, that will, is touched by the Holy Spirit, that person can trust Christ if they only will. The man with 6,000 devils could still come to Jesus, **"But when he saw Jesus afar off, he ran and worshipped him"** (Mark 5:6).

What that tells me is that all the devils in the world can't stop a man from coming to Christ if he really wants to. That's why Satan fights the message of the gospel the way he does. It has the power to awaken the heart, **"For I am not ashamed of the gospel of Christ: for it is the power of God unto salvation to every one that believeth"** (Romans 1:16).

Chapter Five – The Christian's Battle

For we wrestle not against flesh and blood, but against principalities, against powers, against the rulers of the darkness of this world, against spiritual wickedness in high places. Wherefore take unto you the whole armour of God, that ye may be able to withstand in the evil day, and having done all, to stand

Ephesians 6:12-13

Satan's attack on the born again child of God is different from his manipulation of the unsaved. There are a couple things that he cannot do to a born again Christian.

First of all, he cannot have your soul. He cannot take nor cause you to lose your salvation. You belong to Christ and are already seated in heavenly places in Him, and for that reason, Satan hates your guts. You used to be on his team. You were a vessel that he could control and use. You were a real team player. He didn't give you much trouble at all in those days.

He had you right where he wanted you. But you went and changed teams. You actually changed families. You were of your father the Devil, and now you're a child of the living God. Can you imagine what he would do to you if God would let him? But that's the wonderful thing; Satan cannot do anything to us that God does not allow.

The next thing Satan nor his minions cannot do to you is possess you. You are a temple of the Holy Ghost. Satan is not going to go up in there with Him.

It would be like, "knock, knock."

"May I help you?"

"Oops, wrong house!"

Satan's line of attack against the believer is external and is aimed at influencing the battle between the Christian's old and new natures, **"For the flesh lusteth against the Spirit, and the Spirit against the flesh: and these are contrary the one to the other: so that ye cannot do the things that ye would"** (Galatians 5:17).

The day you are born again, the battle begins. The body of flesh has been cut loose from your soul, but it's still there, and it still thinks it's alive. It's a zombie – a walking dead man who just won't stay down. The Holy Spirit, who is the Spirit of Christ, God Himself, took up residence in your spirit and gave you a new nature; **"the mind of Christ"** (1 Corinthians 2:16).

These two natures are at war in you. Paul describes that your objective in the battle is that you **"put off concerning the former conversation the old man, which is corrupt according to the deceitful lusts; And**

be renewed in the spirit of your mind; And that ye put on the new man, which after God is created in righteousness and true holiness" (Ephesians 4:22-24).

Your enemies in this war are the Devil, the world, and the flesh. The Devil and his spirits are in the world using the things of the world to provoke your flesh to act.

Those spirits of the air are in your ear 24-7 at a spiritual, subliminal level seeking to plant thoughts in your mind. Subliminal means "below the threshold." Webster's Dictionary offers two definitions; both are applicable. One, "inadequate to produce a sensation or mental awareness." Two, "existing or functioning below the threshold of consciousness."

This has been done in advertising and has been proven to affect thought and behavior. A thought can be placed in your mind without you noticing and manifests later. It just pops into your mind. You think that it's your idea. On the other hand, an audible voice would expose the enemy and be counterproductive to his program.

Remember, none of this is real. We do not exist. One thing that makes this so easy for the enemy is the fact that most of the material he needs to work with is already there in our flesh, in the old man; the old nature. It merely needs to be stirred up or activated.

This is what is called temptation. Paul said, **"For I know that in me (that is, in my flesh,) dwelleth no good thing"** (Romans 7:18).

These spirits are ancient intelligences. They know us better than we know ourselves. They have millennia of experience manipulating us. They know what makes you tick. They know all the right buttons to push.

They want you to walk in the flesh, not in the spirit. If you are walking in the flesh, not only can God's light not shine through you, but you actually do damage to His cause by being a false witness. This is called your testimony.

Satan cannot have your soul, but he can steal your testimony. He can make you good for nothing if you let him, but you do not have to let him. You have everything that you need to win this battle. If only you will exercise your will to use it.

You are in a war. The sooner that you realize it, the sooner you can begin to fight and win. The story is told of the missionary and the Native American chief who had recently been saved. The chief tells the missionary, "In heart is good dog, bad dog, always fight."

The missionary asked him, "Which one wins?"

The chief answers, "The one I feed."

And so it is, **"For he that soweth to his flesh shall of the flesh reap corruption; but he that soweth to the Spirit shall of the Spirit reap life everlasting"** (Galatians 6:8).

We want the good dog to win, right? But like the prophet said in Hosea 4:6, **"My people are destroyed for lack of knowledge."**

Jesus said, **"It is the spirit that quickeneth; the flesh profiteth nothing: the words that I speak unto you, they are spirit, and they are life"** (John 6:63).

Paul said, **"So then faith cometh by hearing, and hearing by the word of God"** (Romans 10:17).

Peter said, **"As newborn babes, desire the sincere milk of the word, that ye may grow thereby"** (1 Peter 2:2).

And Paul again, **"Christ also loved the church, and gave himself for it; That he might sanctify and cleanse it with the washing of water by the word"** (Ephesians 5:25-26).

Jesus prayed to the Father, **"Sanctify them through thy truth: thy word is truth"** (John 17:17). From the very air around us, we are being constantly bombarded with the voice of the enemy. We need light and truth. The psalmist said, **"The entrance of thy words giveth light"** in Psalm 119:130.

In all the verses we just looked at, the word of God is given as the source of our spiritual growth or sanctification.

Our three-in-one God: Father, Son, and Holy Spirit provided a three-in-one man: body, soul, and spirit, and a three-in-one salvation: *justification, sanctification, and glorification*.

If you've been born again, the first part of your salvation has already happened. It is past tense. It deals with the penalty for sin. This is *justification*.

When you trusted Christ and were born again, a judicial transaction took place in the eyes of God. **"For he hath made him to be sin for us, who knew no sin; that we might be made the righteousness of God in him"** (2 Corinthians 5:21).

Christ's death on the cross was applied to you when we were born again. His blood paid for and cleansed all your sin; past, present and future. He then imputed, or placed on your account, His own sinless righteousness.

This is the great exchange that is justification. He took our sin, and we got His righteousness. That is now and forever your standing before God. As the Lord said, **"It is finished"** (John 19:30).

Sanctification is the part of your salvation that you are involved in right now. It means "set apart for a holy purpose." It is present tense. Justification was an event. Sanctification is an event that leads to a process.

At the moment of your justification, you were sanctified, and the process began. Sanctification deals with the power of sin in your life now. In sanctification, we are being **"conformed to the image of his son"** (Romans 8:29).

Paul describes the process in 2 Corinthians 3:17-18, **"Now the Lord is that Spirit: and where the Spirit of the Lord is, there is liberty. But we all, with open face beholding as in a glass the glory of the Lord, are changed into the same image from glory to glory, even as by the Spirit of the Lord."**

The same Holy Spirit who saved and sealed us when we were born again and justified is now at work in us to make us like Jesus. **"For it is God which worketh in you both to will and to do of his good pleasure"** (Philippians 2:13).

The third part of our salvation is *glorification*. It is the future tense and deals with the very presence of sin. Glorification will take place at the coming of Jesus Christ to gather his church. We will be changed.

We will receive new bodies that are sinless and eternal, just like the one Jesus rose from the dead in. We will then be 100% sinless in spirit, soul, and body for all of eternity. This is our blessed hope, and we will examine that in a later chapter.

Back to sanctification and the Bible's role in the process. God's full and final revelation of Himself to us is the Bible. You are only ever going to know God to the extent that you know his word.

The words of the Holy Spirit on the pages of the Holy Bible are the only 100% pure and holy thing on this earth. These words will cleanse you, purify you, teach you, build you up, correct you, arm you, equip you, mature you, protect you, and bring a peace and a joy in your heart that this world knows nothing about. These words are spirit, and they will feed your spirit **"until Christ be formed in you"** (Galatians 4:19).

Everything you need to grow in grace is in that Book. The Devil will do everything in his power to keep you from living in that Book. Peter said:

> **Grace and peace be multiplied unto you through the knowledge of God, and of Jesus our Lord, According as his divine power hath given unto us all things that pertain unto life and godliness, through the knowledge of him that hath called us to glory and virtue: Whereby are given unto us exceeding great and precious promises: that by these ye might be**

> **partakers of the divine nature, having escaped the corruption that is in the world through lust** (2 Peter 1:2-4).

That is sanctification. Ignorance of the Bible is ignorance of God. Do you want all things that pertain unto life and godliness? Do you want God's exceeding great and precious promises? Do you want to be a partaker of the divine nature? Do you want to escape the corruption that is in the world? Well, then you must have knowledge of Him.

The Bible isn't a book. It is the Book. You can't put that Book in too high of a place. David said, "thou hast magnified thy word above all thy name" in Psalm 138:2.

If you think I'm overstressing a point, listen to what Peter says about the scriptures.

> **For we have not followed cunningly devised fables, when we made known unto you the power and coming of our Lord Jesus Christ, but were eyewitnesses of his majesty. For he received from God the Father honour and glory, when there came such a voice to him from the excellent glory, This is my beloved Son, in whom I am well pleased. And this voice which came**

from heaven we heard, when we were with him in the holy mount (2 Peter 1:16-18).

What Peter is referring to is an event recorded in Matthew 17, Mark 9, and Luke 9. It is called the Mount of Transfiguration. It is truly a close encounter of the God kind. What you have here is God the Son momentarily transfigured and revealing the eternal glory. You also have God the Father speaking from heaven and the Holy Spirit manifesting in a bright cloud.

This is about as up close and personal as you could get to God, wouldn't you think? But look at what 2 Peter 1:19 says next, **"We have also a more sure word of prophecy; whereunto ye do well that ye take heed."**

What? More sure? What could he be talking about? More sure than God the Son transfigured right before your eyes? More sure than the voice of God the Father speaking to you from heaven? More sure than a manifestation of the Shekinah glory? Wow! What could it be? Read on. **"Knowing this first, that no prophecy of the scripture is of any private interpretation. For the prophecy came not in old time by the will of man: but holy men of God spake as they were moved by the Holy Ghost"** (verses 20-21).

The scripture. Peter is talking about the Bible. Peter says that Book is a more sure word of God than anything that happened on the Mount of Transfiguration and here is why.

Experiences can fade. Memories can play tricks on you, but one thing won't, **"For all flesh is as grass, and all the glory of man as the flower of grass. The grass withereth, and the flower thereof falleth away: But the word of the Lord endureth for ever. And this is the word which by the gospel is preached unto you"** (1 Peter 1:24-25).

The scripture is of no private interpretation, unlike a story or an experience. Like the God who wrote it, it is the same yesterday, today, and forever.

When you fill yourself up with His words you have filled yourself up with His Spirit and with Him. Listen, please. Are you saved? Have you been born again? If so, how did that happen? **"Being born again, not of corruptible seed, but of incorruptible, by the word of God, which liveth and abideth for ever"** (1 Peter 1:23).

You got born again by the words of that Book. You are never going to know the Lord like you want to know Him without knowing the Bible. You may ask this point shouldn't we be talking more about prayer? Surely that is just as important as Bible study.

Okay pray to whom? Pray about what? On what grounds? You're never going to have an effective prayer life without first living in that Book. Effective prayer is praying in the will of God by the Spirit of God to the heart of God. You need the word of God to know about any of that.

Jesus said, **"for without me ye can do nothing"** (John 15:5). The Lord Himself when tempted by Satan in the wilderness answered each of the three temptations with "it is written." That's how it is done.

What would Jesus do? He would live in that Book. In describing the Christian spiritual armor Paul gives five pieces of defensive covering but only one weapon, **"the sword of the Spirit, which is the word of God"** (Ephesians 6:17).

The writer of Hebrews describes this weapon, the word of God, as **"quick, and powerful, and sharper than any twoedged sword, piercing even to the dividing asunder of soul and spirit, and of the joints and marrow, and is a discerner of the thoughts and intents of the heart"** (Hebrews 4:12). You will get slaughtered on the battlefield without your weapon.

Every time, for sure, you can count on it, the Devil wants to separate you from your sword. This has been his line of attack since his very first encounter with mankind. The serpent's first words to Eve were **"yea,**

hath God said" (Genesis 3:10). His first attack was on the words of God.

God told Adam that there was only one rule in the garden and that if he broke that rule **"thou shalt surely die"** (Genesis 2:17). Satan steps in and says, **"ye shall not surely die"** (Genesis 3:4).

It has been around 6,000 years since those words were spoken and Satan is still telling the same lie. Paul warned the church in Corinth, **"But I fear, lest by any means, as the serpent beguiled Eve through his subtilty, so your minds should be corrupted from the simplicity that is in Christ"** (2 Corinthians 11:3).

Remember the Parable of the Sower? Jesus said that the seed was the word of God and that as soon as it was sown **"the fowls of the air came and devoured it up"** (Mark 4:4).

Jesus then identifies the fowls of the air as being the wicked one and Satan, and reveals their objective in Luke 8:12, **"then cometh the devil, and taketh away the word out of their hearts, lest they should believe and be saved."**

Satan is not changed. This is still his number one job – attacking the words of God. So, if you're not saved, or are saved but not living in that Book, you now know who is controlling your life.

You may be a nice person. That doesn't bother the Devil as long as you stay out of that Book. You may go to church. That won't bother him either if you're not living in that Book. If you're not living in that Book, you'll be walking in darkness.

No matter how good your life may seem to you the Devil has you right where he wants you. If you are not in that Book every day, then you are not filled with God's word. You have no light or truth to affect the dark world around you.

No matter how fine your life may seem to you, you're a spiritual failure. As things go in the spiritual realm it all comes down to you, Christian. If you cannot walk in victory in the battle between your flesh and spirit, then you will have no impact on the world around you and people will not get the word of God.

God asks you, **"How then shall they call on him in whom they have not believed? and how shall they believe in him of whom they have not heard? and how shall they hear without a preacher? And how shall they preach, except they be sent?"** (Romans 10:14-15).

God calls and sends you as ambassadors for Christ, **"as though God did beseech you by us: we pray you in Christ's stead, be ye reconciled to God"** (2 Corinthians 5:20).

This cannot be done in the flesh by our own strength. This is a work of the Holy Spirit working through a person who is filled with and walking in the Spirit. It's up to you.

They will not seek they must be sought. They will not come, they must be brought. They will not learn, they must be taught. Are you ready to get out of the way and let God work through you?

The Bible tells you how all things that pertain to life and godliness. Romans chapter 6 gives you the path to spiritual victory. Paul starts the chapter off with the situation in the form of a question, **"What shall we say then? Shall we continue in sin, that grace may abound?"**

Paul had just explained all the wonders of justification in the fifth chapter leading up to this question. An accurate description of God's grace and justification naturally raises this question. Justification just sounds too good to be true.

People will ask**, "so, now that I'm saved can I just do anything I want and still go to heaven?"** Paul says that he often got the same response, **"And not rather, (as we be slanderously reported, and as some affirm that we say,) Let us do evil, that good may come? whose damnation is just"** (Romans 3:8).

Peter wrote of a similar situation in 2 Peter 3:15-16, **"the longsuffering of our Lord is salvation; even as**

our beloved brother Paul also according to the wisdom given unto him hath written unto you; As also in all his epistles, speaking in them of these things; in which are some things hard to be understood, which they that are unlearned and unstable wrest, as they do also the other scriptures, unto their own destruction."

New Testament salvation is a free gift of grace and happens the moment that a person is born again. This is foolishness to the natural man. Human reasoning and experience say you must earn it. There's no such thing as a free lunch.

The only thing that human pride hates to hear more than *there is something that you have to do* is hearing that *there's nothing that you can do*. So, we can understand where the question comes from. Shall we continue in sin? If you're not living in that Book how in the world do you answer that question? There are truths in God's word that bring light and result in victory.

Victory comes through a knowledge of God's word applied. Watch as we return to Romans 6. The question in verse 1: **"Shall we continue in sin?"** The answer in verse 2: **"God forbid."** The explanation is in verse 3: **"Know ye not?"** It says to overcome sin, God made a way you have to know it: **"Know ye not, that so many of us as were baptized into Jesus Christ were baptized into his death?"**

Baptized, immersed, plunged, absorbed by the Holy Spirit into the universal spiritual body of Christ; not talking about water here. We were placed in Christ therefore, **"Knowing this, that our old man is crucified with him, that the body of sin might be destroyed, that henceforth we should not serve sin"** (verse 6).

That body of sins of the flesh is crucified with Christ and no longer has power over me. That's why Paul qualified, **"God forbid. How shall we, that are dead to sin, live any longer therein?"** (Romans 6:2). That is the truth, praise God! And you have to know it because **"the truth shall make you free"** (John 8:32).

That's step one to know. The next step is now that you know you can make it so. Paul uses the word reckon. **"Likewise reckon ye also yourselves to be dead indeed unto sin"** (Romans 6:11).

Reckon is a great word. In the old westerns a cowboy would say, "well I reckon." It means to be of the considered opinion or to take into account. Now that you know you can reckon it so.

You have to know before you can reckon. It does not help you to have a million dollars in the bank if you do not know about it. You may say at this point, "this body of sin sure doesn't feel dead to me." Sure it doesn't. It's not a matter of feelings. It is a matter of fact.

God said that your flesh is crucified with Christ. Period. End of discussion. That is the truth. You must take it on faith, and faith comes from the word of God. It is **"the evidence of things not seen"** (Hebrews 11:1).

Faith is giving God the benefit of the doubt despite all evidence to the contrary. Consider this: If you are saved, at some point in time you were told that a Jewish man died on a cross 2,000 years ago and, because of that, you will go to heaven when you die.

You didn't see that. You didn't feel that. You trusted what the Bible said on the matter and based the destiny of your eternal soul on that. God asked you to believe the same thing about the crucifixion of your flesh that you believed about the forgiveness of your sin.

God said it. That settles it. Now reckon it so. Now, once we put the old man in his place, what then? That is the third and the final step. Yield.

"Neither yield ye your members as instruments of unrighteousness unto sin: but yield yourselves unto God, as those that are alive from the dead, and your members as instruments of righteousness unto God" (Romans 6:13).

Yield to the Holy Spirit within. Be filled with the Spirit. Be led by the Spirit. Walk in the spirit. Submit and surrender. Let Jesus take the wheel. Let Him be the wind in your sails. Listen to his still small voice. Guess where He will lead you.

You got it – to live in that Book. So, three steps to victory. Know that you are crucified with Christ, reckon it so, and yield to the Holy Spirit.

It's all in the Book. **"Hear the word of the Lord, ye that tremble at his word"** (Isaiah 66:5). The Devil and his minions are going to do everything in their power to defile your thoughts. You must fight back on purpose.

"(For the weapons of our warfare are not carnal, but mighty through God to the pulling down of strong holds; Casting down imaginations, and every high thing that exalteth itself against the knowledge of God, and bringing into captivity every thought to the obedience of Christ" (2 Corinthians 10:4-5).

"[W]hatsoever things are true, whatsoever things are honest, whatsoever things are just, whatsoever things are pure, whatsoever things are lovely, whatsoever things are of good report; if there be any virtue, and if there be any praise, think on these things" (Philippians 4:8).

"Speaking to yourselves in psalms and hymns and spiritual songs, singing and making melody in your heart to the Lord" (Ephesians 5:19).

We have to concentrate on doing it until it becomes a habit in our lives. This is the sanctification process.

This is spiritual growth. Jesus said, **"ye are the salt of the earth"** and **"ye are the light of the world"** (Matthew 5:13a, 14a). The Holy Spirit in the Christian is who draws people to Christ.

He can pierce the darkness, touch the heart of an unsaved person, and show them their need. This is how the Father draws men to Christ. **"No man can come to me, except the Father which hath sent me draw him"** (John 6:44).

Some few will respond to that light and come to Christ. Sadly, most will not, because **"this is the condemnation, that light is come into the world, and men loved darkness rather than light, because their deeds were evil"** (John 3:19).

Some people, when repeatedly exposed to the light of the gospel, gradually come under conviction and believe on Christ. Others harden their heart more and more and never do. Only God knows who is whom. As long as we are living in that Book and allowing the Holy Spirit to work through us, we have done our job.

One way or the other, we've been faithful and true witnesses. It is not so much a matter of what we do,

it's a matter of who we are. If we will only yield to Him, we will be who He wants us to be. **"For this is the will of God, even your sanctification"** (1 Thessalonians 4:3).

Chapter Six – Spirits of Fear

For God hath not given us the spirit of fear; but of power, and of love, and of a sound mind

2 Timothy 1:7

As we talked about earlier, the fleshly body is a veil that hides the spiritual realm from our natural senses. God can remove the veil when He so desires, and the Bible contains many accounts of Him doing so. There are times, however, when the fleshly veil is damaged or weakened and begins to fail.

In times of such extremity, such as sleep deprivation, starvation, disease, near death, and psychotropic drug use, the spiritual realm can begin to bleed through into a person's perception. People have visions. They hear voices.

These are not necessarily hallucinations, though some may be. The Bible says that there is a spiritual realm inhabited by spiritual beings all around us. So, there is.

The opinions of secular science and medicine do not alter the truth. Most people with serious mental issues hear voices and claim that those voices cause their bad behavior.

These people have some disease or damage to the function or chemistry of their brain that puts them in a place that you or I could only reach by doing methamphetamines for two weeks with no food or sleep. Unfortunately, I can speak to that from a place of personal experience.

Over many years of serious hardcore drug use, I have been to that place many times. When I talk to mentally ill people and they describe to me what they are experiencing, it is the same thing. I knew what I had done to myself at those times, and why I was seeing and hearing things.

Imagine the torment of waking up every day, not being on drugs, and still seeing and hearing things. These sinister entities know and love when someone is starting to perceive them. They are vicious, cruel, and sadistic.

They love your fear. They toy with you. They know things about you. They can impersonate people. They torture, torment, and play with you. Certain medications can help turn down the volume by treating what is wrong with these people's brains.

In the course of my ministry over the last decade, I have come to know a few men with serious mental issues. Some of these men have been driven to kill by the voices. These men are all in prison; some for murder.

All of them shared with me that the voices drove them to do whatever it was that they were in prison for. The

Bible says that **"fear hath torment"** (1 John 4:18). This torment can drive a person to do crazy and terrible things. The little devils just laugh and laugh. You are entertainment. I have observed something wonderful happen in the lives of these men when they come to know Christ.

When you don't know what the voices are, they terrify you. The unknown is what is so debilitating. When you fear them, they torment you and make normal functioning impossible.

When you can show a believer who is hearing voices just what and who these voices are, it is life changing. Remember, these spirits are disembodied. They can't hurt you.

They are nothing but little winged whisperers. They're little big mouths – all bark and no bite. You can flick them away with your finger. They are nothing but sidekicks of a defeated foe, just waiting to take a long swim in a lake of fire.

They are nothing and certainly nothing to fear. Annoying? Yes, but no big deal. Like a naughty child, start talking back to them about the blood of Jesus Christ and see if that doesn't lessen their desire for conversation.

This is a good illustration of the difference. Imagine you're in a dark room trying to do your job or some complicated tasks and you have what you think is a huge monster hanging over you, growling in your ear. You're not going to be able to function under these conditions.

Now turn on the light in the room and see that the huge scary monster is actually a little kid in a Halloween mask. Is he still there? Yes. Is he annoying? Yes.

Is he scary? No, and you can function just fine. I have personally seen this work in several men's lives in prison where I was ministering. These men just were not scared or tormented by the voices anymore.

I'm not a medical doctor. I wouldn't tell anybody to go off their meds. Each individual has to work with their medical doctor as far as volume control goes, but when the voices do come back, and they do, those believers who know what they are never have to fear them again or allow them to affect their behavior.

I brought all that up to re-emphasize just how real the spiritual world is. While the mentally ill experience demonic activity on a conscious level, and most people only experience them on a subliminal level, the fact of their presence and effect is the same. This is very real.

They do exist. They plant thoughts in your mind constantly. As Christians, we need the constant spiritual cleansing of the Word of God.

Your mind gets muddied by contact with this filthy world. Picture your mind as a glass of muddy water. Picture the Word of God as a pitcher of clear, pure water. Start pouring it in that glass of muddy water. Keep pouring. What happens? You get it.

We need that all the time. These voices never stop. Our flesh never stops fighting for its lusts.

I am convinced that we start each day a lap behind in the race. By the time I'm done in the bathroom and start making coffee, that flesh has been up and running for 10 minutes.

One of my mentors taught me this, **"Let everything that hath breath praise the LORD"** (Psalm 150:6). Chaps said that as soon as he wakes up, he takes a deep breath and praises the Lord. I do that too now.

It works. Just like the guys hearing the voices audibly, we identify the source and reality of them. We can begin to see their effect on our thoughts.

These voices are constantly tempting us as Christians to act in the flesh from self, contrary to the will of God, to live independently of the control of the Holy Spirit. Every man is tempted when he is drawn away of his own lusts and enticed. **"Then when lust hath conceived, it bringeth forth sin: and sin, when it is finished, bringeth forth death"** (James 1:15).

Paul describes his struggle in Romans 7:20-23:

> **Now if I do that I would not, it is no more I that do it, but sin that dwelleth in me. I find then a law, that, when I would do good, evil is present with me. For I delight in the law of God after the inward man: But I see another law in my members, warring against the law of my mind, and bringing me into captivity to the law of sin which is in my members.**

We are constantly being tempted by an enemy outside of ourselves who is trying to stir up the sin nature that we still carry. We must be on guard. James promised, **"Submit yourselves therefore to God. Resist the devil, and he will flee from you"** (James 4:7).

I have heard people dismiss demonic activity, saying that that is not the devil; that is just the flesh. Who do they think is tempting the flesh? Our battle is against the devil, the world, and the flesh. They all work together. Let us look at temptation.

"Love not the world, neither the things that are in the world. If any man love the world, the love of the Father is not in him. For all that is in the world, the

lust of the flesh, and the lust of the eyes, and the pride of life, is not of the Father, but is of the world" (1 John 2:15-16).

The *lust of the flesh* is the desires of the body; the cravings for sensation and pleasure. These are good things perverted, like the sex drive and hunger.

The *lust of the eyes* is covetousness, greediness, materialism, and the love of money.

The *pride of life* is the pride of Satan. It is the desire to be your own God; to live independently of God.

Notice how each lust tempts a different part of the man. The flesh is after the body, the eyes are after the soul, and pride is after the spirit. Satan ran all three on Eve, **"And when the woman saw that the tree was good for food, and that it was pleasant to the eyes, and a tree to be desired to make one wise"** (Genesis 3:6).

Adam and Eve were tempted in spirit, soul, and body, and failed. The Lord Jesus Christ, **"the last Adam"** (1 Corinthians 15:45), passes all three temptations in the wilderness.

In Matthew chapter 4, Jesus hadn't eaten in 40 days. He was hungry. The Devil said, **"command that these stones be made bread"** (verse 3) - the lust of the flesh. The devil then tempted Him to act presumptuously, and jump off the temple, testing God (verse 6) – the pride of life. Finally, the devil showed Him all the kingdoms of the world, said, **"all these things will I give thee, if thou will fall down and worship me"** (verses 8-9) – the lust of the eyes.

This last Adam is **"the Lord from heaven"** (1 Corinthians 15:47), **"But made himself of no reputation, and took upon him the form of a servant, and was made in the likeness of men"** (Philippians 2:7).

He, being fully human, stands in the sinner's place, and passes all the temptations that Adam and Eve failed. The Lord Jesus lives a perfect, sinless life. He then credits to your account when you are born again.

He took up residence inside of you by his Holy Spirit, and now you too can pass the tests of temptation through Him. Paul inspires us so that we **"can do all things through Christ which strengtheneth"** us (Philippians 4:13). That is not a cute saying. That is a spiritual reality from the Word of God.

The Lord Jesus was in all parts, all points, **"tempted like as we are, yet without sin"** (Hebrews 4:15). It is not sin to be tempted. Paul already told us in Romans 7:17, that **"it is no more I that do it, but sin that dwelleth in me."**

A man once said, "it's not a sin for a bird to land on your head; it's a sin to let him build a nest."

Considering what we now know about that which hath wings, the saying is even more applicable.

Sometimes something will come into our minds that is so wrong that we question how that could possibly even come from us. We can feel shame and guilt for such thoughts. Maybe it didn't come from you. Those are the times that I have no problem saying, "that's the Devil."

So, how does temptation progress to sin? The theological term for this is peccability. It means "the ability to sin." This doctrine presents six steps. Presentation, illumination, debate, desire, decision, and finally action.

Step one is the *presentation* of the wrong idea, object, or suggestions. There is no sin in that. Jesus was presented with all three without sin.

The second step is *illumination*. That is when we receive light concerning the moral nature of what is being presented. There is certainly no sin in that.

The sin begins when a person begins to *debate* about something they have already received *illumination* about. You are already in sin before you even have the *desire* to make the *decision to act*. The difference between the Lord Jesus Christ and Adam and Eve or any other sinner is that when He received illumination on the temptation, He never debated what to do. Because his spirit lives in you, you can do the same thing.

We just have to yield to the Holy Spirit when He illuminates that thing, whatever it is. We need to be quick on the draw with our **"get thee hence Satan"** and **"it is written."** Amen.

Chapter Seven – The Voice of God

The words of the Lord are pure words: as silver tried in a furnace of earth, purified seven times. Thou shalt keep them, O Lord, thou shalt preserve them from this generation for ever

Psalm 12:6-7

I want to make a statement first. I praise God that anybody reads any Bible. There are brethren who believe what I believe about the Bible who would not agree with that statement.

First, let me tell you what I believe, in fact, know about the Bible. Then I will explain why I stand by that statement that I just made. I believe that the King James Bible is the Word of God, containing the words of God, and preserved 100 percent without error by divine providence.

I don't just believe it. I know it for a fact and can demonstrate it in the case of any supposed error that anyone thinks they may have found. I stand on Psalms 12:6-7 that we opened this chapter with.

A Christian must make a decision about whether he or she is going to believe that. God said that His words, w-o-r-d-s, words are perfectly pure and preserved forever. Not the general thoughts, message, or ideas, but each and every word.

So, you either believe in a perfect every-word Bible, or you don't. It's as simple as that. Either God preserved it perfectly Himself, or He left it up to man, random chance, and luck, to almost preserve it, pretty close to what it was when it was first written down.

These are your only two choices. There is no middle ground. I have a perfect Bible.

It is right here in my hand. When I stand before the Lord, if I'm wrong about this, and I'm not, I'll say, "I'm sorry, Lord, I just believed every word." I think that's the safer position.

Also, when you come to the Bible believing every word, God is going to give you way more light and revelation than someone who thinks they are smart enough to correct it. We don't correct the Bible, it corrects us. This is how God gave us a perfect Bible.

God gave the Old Testament scriptures to the Jewish people in Hebrew, their language. He preserved it through the priests and scribes. In the time of Christ and the apostles, the universal language of the known world was Greek because of the empire of Alexander the Great.

The books of the New Testament were written in Greek. They were preserved through believers in the

Bible believing churches. The world went through around 1,000 years of what historians call the "Dark Ages."

The common man did not have the scriptures. The Roman church did not allow people to read them, and it persecuted and executed those who had them. In the 1500s, two things happened that changed everything – the Protestant Reformation and the invention of the printing press.

Much of the world began to read rough translations of the scriptures and came out of the Roman church. During this time, the British empire came to rule much of the known world. The saying was, "the sun never sets on the British empire."

There was a Bible believing king on the throne, and **"where the word of a king is, there is power"** (Ecclesiastes 8:4). If you want a Bible with power, it had better be translated under a king, and even better, a king with a Jewish name. James is Jacob in Hebrew.

God used this king and this nation to take his Hebrew Old Testament and Greek New Testament and put them together in one Bible in the universal language of the end-times on earth, English. That was the year 1611, and that Bible is the King James Authorized Version. This is your perfect, every-word Bible for the world.

"This is the bread which the Lord hath given you to eat" (Exodus 16:15). If you have any doubt, just look at what God did with that Book over the next 400 years. Jesus said, **"Howbeit when he, the Spirit of truth, is come, he will guide you into all truth: for he shall not speak of himself; but whatsoever he shall hear, that shall he speak: and he will shew you things to come. He shall glorify me"** (John 16:13-14).

Nothing on this earth has ever glorified the Lord Jesus Christ more than that old King James Holy Bible.

Jesus also said, **"the tree is known by his fruit"** (Matthew 12:33). Compare the fruit of the King James Bible to the fruit of all the Johnny-come-lately new Bibles put together. It's not even close. There is nothing on earth like the King James Bible. It is perfect.

Next to my relationship with Christ, that's the most wonderful thing I know. And the two are so interconnected that it's hard to tell where they separate. God showed me this truth shortly after I got saved.

I've examined much of what's in print on the subject, all sides of the debate, and nobody has been able to talk me out of believing that Book. As you can probably tell, I'm extremely serious about this subject. But there is one thing more important than having the right Bible.

That is having the right Savior. This goes back to my opening statement. Look, if you found Christ in an NIV, or a Living Bible, or an English Standard, praise God.

Hallelujah! I praise God that anybody reads any Bible. I spent a decade of my ministry and pastorate in prison. I worked at the chapel. Under the chaplain's authority, I was pastor of the Christian church for a 4,000-man prison. In that environment, you get every diverse congregation. You get all types from all backgrounds, carrying all different Bibles, if they were carrying one at all.

There wasn't a man in any one of our congregations who had been there any length of time at all that didn't know what I believe about the King James Bible. But I would never belittle, embarrass, or offend a man coming to church to seek the Lord because he didn't have the right Bible in his hand.

I'll be **"wise as a serpent and harmless as a dove"** (Matthew 10:16). Being crafty, I'll catch you with guile, (2 Corinthians 12:16). Don't spook them. Draw them in easy. Even if they don't come around to my

way of thinking, I'm still going to preach to them, love them, pray with them, and fellowship with them. The chapel is the only church in town in the prison yard.

We want them in church, not back in the unit with the gangs and the drugs. If you run them off from church, the Devil will be happy to take them back. He doesn't care what Bible version is gathering dust on their shelf down in the unit.

I explained it to the men like this, and believe me, that crowd got it. If the Bible is your dope, even watered down or cut dope will still get you high. It will just take more, and the high won't be as good.

But if I know the source, I can get mine pure. I mean right off the boat; right off the brick. I mean, whew, bang, take a hit of that. Yeah, that's the stuff! That's your King James Bible. The 100 percent pure, uncut word of God.

So now you can go back to all those places I talked about living in that Book, and you know exactly what Book I was talking about. As much as I love the Book, Satan hates it more. That is why there are so many new Bible versions out there.

Satan wants to confuse the issue and destroy Christian unity. If something is perfect and you change it, then it's not perfect anymore. That is the problem with the New King James. When they changed words, error was introduced. It's worth learning a few old words in order to have a perfect Bible. Someone will always ask, "well, what about everybody that doesn't speak English?" God only ever gave His word in one language, Hebrew, then Greek, now English.

What people who don't speak one or all of these languages do is what they have always done, translate it into their language or learn English. Much of the world now does speak English as a second language. It is the universal language of the world.

There is to be a standard, a Final Authority for a Bible believer. Their standard and Final Authority is the King James Bible. Anyone else will have for their final authority some Greek or Hebrew scholar's opinion of what they think it should have said. That's a big difference.

"And ye shall be as gods, knowing good and evil" (Genesis 3:5). Man in his pride wants to be his own final authority. That is our main problem.

When we remove the Bible as the Final Authority, when truth has become a matter of opinion and speculation rather than revelation, truth is revealed by God. Truth is reality according to God, not the consensus of human opinion. Satan's first line of attack will always be against the Bible – the voice of God.

God's delivery system for His word is the Church – the Body of Christ. Where Satan can remove the authority of the Bible from the churches, they will fall like dominoes. Apostasy, compromise, and worldliness will put their lights out.

The advances that the enemy has made just in my lifetime are shocking. He has offered a variety of counterfeits in the place of biblical Christianity. The same thing that he pulled off with the Roman church in the Dark Ages, he is doing today.

For much of history, the words Christian and the church brought to mind the Roman Catholic Church. Even today, when you pick up a book on church history, it will be a history of the Roman Catholic Church. The Roman Catholic Church does share some beliefs with biblical Christianity, but it is in no way a representation of Christian belief and practice in the Bible.

This was the reason for the Protestant Reformation. The Reformation was a back-to-the-Bible movement, so the Devil holds out the Roman church in his hand and says, "this is Christianity." Many people say, "no thanks."

Today, the Devil is holding out more counterfeits in his hand and saying, "this is Christianity." There is an absolute avalanche of nonsense coming over the airwaves, promoted by slick con men called "Christian" celebrities. They are peddling a false gospel of satisfying and entertaining self.

It's all glitz and glitter and dollar signs. It is a carnival atmosphere of indulgence and emotional experience.

There is no talk of sin and death and hell and repentance.

It is carnal, worldly, sensual, and devilish. When you say "Christian" these days, this is the stuff that people think that you're talking about. Ask most people what they know about Jesus and the Bible, and if it isn't anti-Christ propaganda from skeptics and critics, then it's the representation of these apostate churches.

Because most people are completely ignorant of the Bible. They have no idea of what biblical Christianity is or that it even exists. What people are seeing is a show — a fleshly emotionalism masquerading as the Holy Spirit, nonsensical babbling being called a gift of the Spirit, give-to-get covetousness sold like lottery tickets, phony healing lines working widows out of their savings, con men behind pulpits selling holy oil, holy water, holy hankies, and a whole gift shop of tourist trinkets. This is the fruit of all your new modern "easy-to-read" Bibles.

Without a Final Authority, anything goes. The Devil can slip anything in right under your noses. Biblical Christianity is under fierce attack on many fronts.

In upcoming chapters, we will look at some of the false teachings that the devil has slipped in that do damage to the gospel of grace and the Body of Christ. The bad teachings that the Devil has slipped into the Body of Christ are designed to take our eyes off of

Christ and His finished work and get us to focus on self, our works, our feelings, our emotions, our health, and our prosperity. In true biblical Christianity, we decrease and He increases. It's all about Him, not us.

Chapter Eight - Father and Master

I Am the man that hath seen affliction by the rod of his wrath

Lamentations 3:1

God dealt with you as a sinner on the cross in Christ. You are crucified with Christ; already seated in heavenly places in Christ Jesus. Because you were made the righteousness of God in Him, that is your standing before God.

You have been justified, just as if you had never sinned. This justified standing makes you a child of God. That is your relationship to God that can never change.

God is dealing with you now as a son – one of his own children. This has to do with your daily walk or fellowship with God, your actual state, and the state of your fellowship. Your standing, like your relationship, never changes.

Your state, like your fellowship, depends on your daily walk and does change. This is where you are in the sanctification process. One of my first pastors, Dr. C.R. Williams, told me this, "Brother Roy, a Christian, has two ships. His first ship is his relationship to God. That's the one that takes him to heaven. The other ship is his fellowship with God. That's the one that keeps him happy on the way there."

I never forgot that.

Every day, God is ordering the events of your life to get you in the right state. It is much better when we recognize that and submit. **"For if we would judge ourselves, we should not be judged. But when we are judged, we are chastened of the Lord, that we should not be condemned with the world"** (1 Corinthians 11:31-32).

To yield and submit is simple. **"If we confess our sins, he is faithful and just to forgive us our sins, and to cleanse us from all unrighteousness"** (1 John 1:9).

Both of these verses are talking about your daily walk and fellowship with your Father. They are talking about your state, not your unchanging standing.

"For whom the Lord loveth he chasteneth, and scourgeth every son whom he receiveth" (Hebrews 12:6). Thank God for His tough love, because where God refuses to correct, there He has decided to destroy.

There is no man nearer the flames of hell than the man God is done wasting his time on. **"As many as I love, I rebuke and chasten: be zealous therefore, and repent"** (Revelation 3:19).

Think about it. All the tribulation that you go through in this life is all the hell that you will ever experience. Death for the Christian is an end to all of that and a doorway to glory.

Consider the unsaved. All the fleeing happiness that they experience in this life will be all the heaven that they will ever know. Death for them will be the end of all that and a doorway to eternal fire.

Thank God for your tribulations. Thank God for the fire here and now. **"Behold, I have refined thee, but not with silver; I have chosen thee in the furnace of affliction"** (Isaiah 48:10). When the fire is put to the pot, all the garbage comes to the top.

So, it is when God's chastening tries our souls. When we go through the fire, all the garbage in our lives that is not of God will reveal itself in our hearts. The fire is there for a reason.

Hebrews 12:10 contrasts our natural father's chastening with that of our heavenly father, **"For they verily for a few days chastened us after their own pleasure; but he for our profit, that we might be partakers of his holiness."**

When He wills poverty, poverty is better than riches. And when God wills death, death is better than life. Because God is wisdom itself, He knows what is best. Because He is goodness itself, He cannot do anything but what is best.

Our hearts are hard, proud, selfish, filthy, stubborn, cold, and hypocritical. God must break our hard hearts. He must humble our proud hearts. He must cleanse our filthy hearts. Where the disease is strong, so must be the medicine or the cure will not work.

Jesus is the **"great physician"** (Luke 4:23), and He would never give strong medicine where a weaker one would have worked. The more crooked the piece of iron is, the hotter the flame, and the harder the blows of the hammer will be needed to straighten it out.

Some of us have been crooked for a long time. The fire is there for a reason. What should our response to it be? Look at the life of King David and all that God put him through. Then look at the response of his heart. David's response to all that he had been through was silence without murmuring or complaining. David's silence is an acknowledgment of God as the author of all his afflictions.

David sees through all secondary causes to the primary cause and is silent. Nothing is more important than the primary cause. Nothing can happen that God does not allow.

If you cannot see the hand of God in all things both good and bad that happen to you, your heart will do nothing but worry and complain under affliction. Those who will trust the heart of the Father will see the hand of God in all that comes their way. They will know that it was the great physician that caused them to drink that bitter cure.

They will know that it was love that laid those heavy crosses upon their shoulders. And grace that laid those stripes across their backs. If you think about it, whatever we go through, it is nothing compared to the torments of the damned in hell.

At this very moment, many of them, when they were in this world, never sinned nearly as much as we have, and they are now screaming for all eternity. But for us, **"his anger endureth but a moment; in his favour is life: weeping may endure for a night, but joy cometh in the morning"** (Psalm 30:5).

"Eye hath not seen, nor ear heard, neither have entered into the heart of man, the things which God hath prepared for them that love him" (1 Corinthians 2:9).

Anything and everything we endure in this short life in comparison with the glories of heaven are less than a mosquito bite, **"For I reckon that the sufferings of this present time are not worthy to be compared with the glory which shall be revealed in us"** (Romans 8:18).

David said in Psalm 119:71, **"it is good for me that I have been afflicted."** The obedient child gives themselves up to God as a living sacrifice.

The heart yielded to the Holy Spirit says, "Lord, here I am. Do with me what you will. I give myself up to you. So, strike, Lord, strike and spare not, for I submit to your will. You have a greater interest in me than I have in myself, and therefore I surrender to you. Take me, break me, make me."

To my soul I say, "soul, do not murmur, do not question. I command you, soul, to be silent under the chastening hand of God. Stop all complaining and be silent." God always has reasons for what He does, yet He does not have to show us those reasons.

I remember the account of a missionary sister in Africa. Soldiers attacked the mission, killed the men, and tortured and raped the women for months. This sister survived and related the question that God spoke to her heart in the midst of her torment. He asked her, "Can you thank me for trusting you with this experience, even though I may never tell you why?" Now, that's biblical Christianity.

You will be hard pressed to find that on your so-called Christian TV programs. Jesus said, **"If any man will come after me, let him deny himself, and take up his cross, and follow me"** (Matthew 16:24).

This is God dealing with us as his children in this life. There is a day coming when we will be dealt with as His servants, **"for we shall all stand before the judgment seat of Christ"** (Romans 14:10).

Just as the Bible talks about **"sorer punishment"** (Hebrews 10:29) and **"greater damnation"** (Matthew 23:14) for the unsaved in hell, we are also told of greater reward in eternity for the saved. That reward will be based on your service to Him in this life.

Heaven will be better for some than for others. Some will shine brighter, **"for one star differeth from another star in glory. So also is the resurrection of the dead"** (1 Corinthians 15:41b-42a).

"Then shall the righteous shine forth as the sun in the kingdom of their father" (Matthew 13:43). Jesus said, **"let your light so shine before men, that they may see your good works, and glorify your Father which is in heaven"** (Matthew 5:16).

How bright you shine in eternity will depend on how bright you shine on earth. **"And he said unto him, Well, thou good servant: because thou hast been faithful in a very little, have thou authority over ten cities"** (Luke 19:17).

How many cities will you light up for Him in the kingdom? In this world now, **"we wrestle not against flesh and blood, but against principalities, against powers, against the rulers of the darkness of this world, against spiritual wickedness in high places"** (Ephesians 6:12). These demonic powers cover the world in darkness for their master, Satan.

In the kingdom, we **"are as the angels of God in heaven"** (Matthew 22:30). We replace those demonic princes and rule and illuminate the world with our Savior. We **"shall be priests of God and of Christ, and shall reign with him a thousand years"** (Revelation 20:6).

"Do ye not know that the saints shall judge the world? Know ye not that we shall judge angels?" (1 Corinthians 6:2a, 3a). We shall judge the world, but first our own service shall be judged. **"For we must all appear before the judgment seat of Christ; that every one may receive the things done in his body, according to that he hath done, whether it be good or bad"** (2 Corinthians 5:10).

This is not the general judgment known as the Great White Throne that happens before eternity begins. This Judgment Seat of Christ is only for the Body of Christ and happens right after the rapture of the Church.

We will study that in detail in the next chapter. Paul describes the Judgment Seat of Christ in 1 Corinthians 3:11-15:

> **For other foundation can no man lay than that is laid, which is Jesus Christ. Now if any man build upon this foundation gold, silver, precious stones, wood, hay, stubble; Every**

man's work shall be made manifest: for the day shall declare it, because it shall be revealed by fire; and the fire shall try every man's work of what sort it is. If any man's work abide which he hath built thereupon, he shall receive a reward. If any man's work shall be burned, he shall suffer loss: but he himself shall be saved; yet so as by fire.

Gold, silver, precious stones; bling. We want all our bling to make it through the fire. That will be our shine through all eternity. We have only one life, and it will soon be passed. Only what's done for Christ will last.

We will stand before Him one day, our Savior, the one who died for you. But He won't be the lowly Galilean on earth. No gentle Jesus, meek and mild. **"Though we have known Christ after the flesh, yet henceforth we know him no more"** (2 Corinthians 5:16). No, you will stand before the glorified risen Lord, King of kings and Lord of lords. Every knee shall bow.

Even John, who wrote six books in the Bible and calls himself, **"the disciple whom Jesus loved"** (John 21:7), **"fell at his feet as dead"** (Revelation 1:17) before God the Son in all His glory. We will be tried by fire in that moment. For our God is a consuming fire.

When He turns his face to you, **"his countenance was as the sun shining in his strength"** (Revelation 1:16). And as He fixes his eyes upon you, they are **"as a flame of fire"** (verse 14).

What works, what service, if any, will be able to withstand that gaze? Most of us on that day will indeed suffer loss.

But praise God, everyone at the Judgment Seat of Christ shall be saved (1 Corinthians 3:15), unlike the Great White Throne, where multitudes are cast into the lake of fire. We will be judged for how useful we were to the Lord in trying to stop as many as possible of that multitude from going to that place.

You are an **"ambassador for Christ,"** according to 2 Corinthians 5:20. What kind of job are you doing? This risen Christ is coming back to the world in blood and fire.

One thing a kingdom always does before it goes to war is recall its ambassadors. That could happen any day, any time. Be ready.

Stay ready. And you won't have to get ready. His coming to gather his Church, his body, to Himself, is our **"blessed hope"** (Titus 2:13).

Chapter Nine – Our Blessed Hope

Looking for that blessed hope, and the glorious appearing of the great God and our Saviour Jesus Christ

Titus 2:13

As a child of God, living in the word of God, we operate in an absolute confidence and assurance. We have hope – not a nebulous wish upon a star kind of hope, but a definitive expectation of that which God has revealed in His word.

This thought should always dictate our behavior. What has God revealed in his word? **"Surely the Lord God will do nothing, but he revealeth his secret unto his servants the prophets"** (Amos 3:7).

Jesus said, **"And now I have told you before it come to pass, that, when it is come to pass, ye might believe"** (John 14:29).

It almost doesn't seem fair, does it? You can read the end of the Book and know how everything turns out. Spoiler alert – we win. And therein lies hope.

When you have a clear picture of the victory that is just around the corner, you can hold on in hope no matter what you are going through. The Bible is one-third prophecy; history written in advance. That is absolute scientific proof of its supernatural origin.

Whoever wrote the Book exists outside of the construct of time. So, He is everywhere and every when. He is omnipresent. He knows everything, even what has not happened yet. He is omniscient and He controls the outcome of everything. He is omnipotent.

That can be nobody but the one true and living God. He told Isaiah, **"I have declared the former things from the beginning; and they went forth out of my mouth, and I shewed them; I did them suddenly, and they came to pass. Because I knew that thou art obstinate, and thy neck is an iron sinew, and thy brow brass; I have even from the beginning declared it to thee; before it came to pass I shewed it thee: lest thou shouldest say, Mine idol hath done them"** (Isaiah 48:3).

Basically, what God said there is, "you want to know who is talking to you? Okay, here's what I'll do. I'll tell you everything that is going to happen before it happens, so that when it happens, you will know that this is me, God."

Not believing the Book is mental illness with a spiritual cause. But the child of God can say with assurance, **"I am not ashamed: for I know whom I have believed, and am persuaded that he is able to keep that which I have committed unto him against that day"** (2 Timothy 1:12).

"Against that day." What day is that? That's the day Christ comes for his Bride, his Body, the Church. 1 Thessalonians 4:13-18 states:

> **But I would not have you to be ignorant, brethren, concerning them which are asleep, that ye sorrow not, even as others which have no hope. For if we believe that Jesus died and rose again, even so them also which sleep in Jesus will God bring with him. For this we say unto you by the word of the Lord, that we which are alive and remain unto the coming of the Lord shall not prevent them which are asleep. For the Lord himself shall descend from heaven with a shout, with the voice of the archangel, and with the trump of God: and the dead in Christ shall rise first: Then we which are alive and remain shall be caught up together with them in the clouds, to meet the Lord in the air: and so shall we ever be with the Lord. Wherefore comfort one another with these words.**

This the Christian's blessed hope. It's not just going to heaven when we die. This is the glorification of the believer. This is where every member of the Body of

Christ since his resurrection receives their resurrection bodies. This is where every born again Christian is gathered together with the Lord to be with Him forever.

This is what we are waiting for. And not just we who are alive, the dead in Christ, them which sleep in Jesus, they are waiting for that day too. Their souls are waiting in heaven with Christ.

This event is called "the rapture." It is not to be confused with the general resurrection of the righteous Old Testament saints. That resurrection happens at the end of the tribulation period when Christ returns to earth in power and glory to set up His thousand-year kingdom.

Why does that matter? Because what you are expecting will affect your behavior while you're waiting for whatever it is. We have a blessed hope. We are waiting for Him, not hell on earth. That's the tribulation.

Paul told Timothy, **"Study to shew thyself approved unto God, a workman that needeth not to be ashamed, rightly dividing the word of truth"** (2 Timothy 2:15). There are some right divisions in the Bible.

If you want to know how to put all the pieces together right, you must be like the believers in Berea of whom Paul said, **"These were more noble than those in**

Thessalonica, in that they received the word with all readiness of mind, and searched the scriptures daily, whether those things were so" (Acts 17:11).

You must study and rightly divide the word of truth for yourself. Paul gives an example of why in 2 Timothy 2:16-18, **"But shun profane and vain babblings: for they will increase unto more ungodliness. And their word will eat as doth a canker: of whom is Hymenaeus and Philetus; Who concerning the truth have erred, saying that the resurrection is past already; and overthrow the faith of some."**

These two false teachers were teaching error concerning the blessed hope, and it was overthrowing the faith of some. Paul was not afraid to call them out by name.

The Devil was trying to slip something in. He has slipped a lot of stuff into the churches over the centuries. Here's an example of rightly dividing scripture when it comes to the subject of the rapture of the church: Your blessed hope.

There are many views and opinions about Christ's second coming. The Devil is always trying to slip something in. Context will determine content when it comes to understanding your Bible. Let's look at

the larger context of the subject in light of the whole Bible, then come back to what Paul says in Thessalonians.

The Old Testament clearly revealed the promise of the resurrection. Job, the oldest book in the Bible, says, **"For I know that my redeemer liveth, and that he shall stand at the latter day upon the earth: And though after my skin worms destroy this body, yet in my flesh shall I see God"** (Job 19:25-26).

This latter day resurrection was also known to Israel through the prophets. **"Behold, O my people, I will open your graves, and cause you to come up out of your graves, and bring you into the land of Israel"** (Ezekiel 37:12).

Notice verse 9 of the same chapter. **"Thus saith the Lord God; Come from the four winds, O breath, and breathe upon these slain, that they may live."** This is almost exactly what Jesus says in Matthew 24:31, **"And he shall send his angels with a great sound of a trumpet, and they shall gather together his elect from the four winds."** These elect are the elect of Isaiah 45:4, **"Israel mine elect."**

Ezekiel is just as specific in verse 11 of chapter 37, **"these bones are the whole house of Israel,"** and more details are revealed in verse 21, **"I will take the children of Israel from among the heathen, whither they be gone, and will gather them on every side, and bring them into their own land."**

This is the context of Christ's teachings concerning His second coming in Matthew 24, Mark 13, and Luke 21.

He is speaking of Israel's resurrection and gathering into their promised land. At the time of these teachings, there was no Body of Christ, and nothing about the Body of Christ had yet been revealed.

It was still a mystery. Notice the exclusively Jewish context. **"Them which be in Judea"** (Matthew 24:1), **"The Sabbath day"** (Matthew 24:20), **"Delivering you up to the synagogues"** (Luke 21:12).

In scripture, rightly divided, God deals with three groups of people, **"Give none offense, neither to the Jews, nor to the Gentiles, nor to the church of God"** (1 Corinthians 10:32). If we fail to discern who God is speaking to or about in any portion of scripture, we will not have rightly divided. We will end up with a wrong interpretation. Everything that we have just looked at falls under the heading of prophecy.

Prophecy is that which has been revealed. In contrast, a mystery is that which has not *yet* been revealed. When rightly dividing the word of truth, the most important division in the Bible is that between prophecy and mystery.

Everything having to do with God's dealing with the nation of Israel falls under the subject of prophecy. Everything having to do with the Church or the Body of Christ is the subject of the mystery. Just as all prophecy was given to Moses and the prophets, all revelation of the mystery was given to the Apostle Paul.

Paul tells us that the church, the body of Christ, is a mystery, **"which was kept secret since the world began"** (Romans 16:25). It was **"hid in God"** (Ephesians 3:9) and was **"not made known"** (Ephesians 3:5). It was **"hid from ages and from generations"** (Colossians 1:26), **"Which none of the princes of this world knew: for had they known it, they would not have crucified the Lord of glory"** (1 Corinthians 2:8).

This mystery Body consists of Jew and Gentile, made one in a brand new, previously unrevealed organism.

Prophecy dealt with a kingdom; a political organization established on earth. The mystery reveals a living organism given a position in the heavenlies. Because the gospel of John was written after the revelation of the mystery, it is John who writes about our union with Christ in the new birth.

It is John who tells us about our blessed hope. **"In my Father's house are many mansions: if it were not so, I would have told you. I go to prepare a place for you. And if I go and prepare a place for you, I will come again, and receive you unto myself; that where I am, there ye may be also"** (John 14:2-3).

That is Jesus taking the Church to their mansions in heaven, not gathering Israel to the promised land on earth. The Jews inherit the earth and are heirs of all the earthly promises to Israel that are the subject of prophecy.

The Church shares in the spiritual blessings to Abraham in his seed, Christ, but we do not become part of the nation of Israel. We have a destiny in the heavens that is different from Israel's destiny. Our gathering to Him in heaven is different from Israel's gathering to Him in Jerusalem.

Things that differ are not the same. Just as the Body of Christ was a mystery until revealed by the Apostle Paul, the rapture of the Church was also a mystery until revealed by the Apostle Paul, **"Behold, I shew you a mystery; We shall not all sleep, but we shall all be changed, In a moment, in the twinkling of an eye, at the last trump: for the trumpet shall sound, and the dead shall be raised incorruptible, and we shall be changed"** (1 Corinthians 15:51-52).

This is not the resurrection at Christ's return in power and glory to set up His kingdom. That was not a mystery at all, but this is something newly revealed connected to the Body of Christ.

Now that we see clearly the difference between the resurrection of Israel and the gathering of the Body of

Christ, the teaching on the subject in Thessalonians will be clear.

In 1 Thessalonians, Paul reveals the details of the catching away of the body of Christ. Paul says we are to **"wait for his Son from heaven, whom he raised from the dead, even Jesus, which delivered us from the wrath to come"** (1 Thessalonians 1:10).

We are delivered from the wrath to come.

What is the wrath to come? Right there in the same epistle, it says, **"For yourselves know perfectly that the day of the Lord so cometh as a thief in the night. For when they shall say, Peace and safety; then sudden destruction cometh upon them, as travail upon a woman with child; and they shall not escape. But ye, brethren, are not in darkness, that that day should overtake you as a thief"** (1 Thessalonians 5:2-4).

Notice that sudden destruction comes on *them*, not *us*. That day does not overtake us because we are gone. **"For God hath not appointed us to wrath, but to obtain salvation by our Lord Jesus Christ"** (1 Thessalonians 5:9).

The wrath to come is not for us. How do we miss it? **"For the Lord himself shall descend from heaven with a shout . . . We which are alive and remain**

shall be caught up together with them in the clouds to meet the Lord in the air" (1 Thessalonians 4:16a, 17a).

We are waiting for his Son from heaven to deliver us from the wrath to come. We're not waiting for death, the Antichrist, the tribulation, the new temple, or the revived Roman Empire. We are waiting for the Lord Jesus Christ to show up and take us to our mansions in heaven. The Thessalonians understood all that. The wrath to come was never a mystery.

The Old Testament prophets described it as well. Jesus had just talked about it. He said, **"For then shall be great tribulation, such as was not since the beginning of the world to this time, no, nor ever shall be"** (Matthew 24:21).

This explains why the Thessalonians were so troubled and why Paul wrote 2 Thessalonians.

Between the writing of 1 Thessalonians and 2 Thessalonians, the church in Thessalonica fell under such persecution and was going through such tribulation that someone claiming apostolic authority had written to them saying that they were in the great tribulation or wrath to come.

"[B]e not soon shaken in mind, or be troubled, neither by spirit, nor by word, nor by letter as from us, as that the day of Christ is at hand" (2 Thessalonians 2:2).

They thought they had missed the rapture and were in the tribulation. To set their minds at ease, Paul reminds them of two things which he lists in the first verse of chapter 2. Two events which he deals with separately.

Event number one: the coming of our Lord Jesus Christ. Event number two: our gathering together unto Him. Because the Thessalonians thought they were in the great tribulation and experiencing the wrath to come, Paul speaks to that first.

Event number one, **"for that day shall not come, except there come a falling away first, and that man of sin be revealed, the son of perdition; Who opposeth and exalteth himself above all that is called God, or that is worshipped; so that he as God sitteth in the temple of God, shewing himself that he is God"** (2 Thessalonians 2:3-4).

Paul tells them to relax. **"The Lord Jesus being revealed from heaven with his mighty angels in flaming fire taking vengeance . . . destruction and punish[ment]"** (2 Thessalonians 1:7-9).

The wrath to come that day cannot happen until after the Antichrist is revealed and commits the Abomination of Desolation. This was the subject of prophecy and had been revealed by the prophet Daniel 500 years before.

Now Paul turns to event number two and begins by reminding them of something he had already revealed to them in person and epistle. Something related to the mystery that was not in Daniel or any of the other prophets' writings. **"Remember ye not, that, when I was yet with you, I told you these things?"** (2 Thessalonians 2:5).

He reminds them that something was holding back the revelation of the Antichrist, **"And now ye know what withholdeth that he might be revealed in his time. For the mystery of iniquity doth already work: only he who now letteth will let, until he be taken out of the way. And then shall that Wicked be revealed, whom the Lord shall consume with the spirit of his mouth, and shall destroy with the brightness of his coming"** (2 Thessalonians 2:6-8).

That "he" who is holding back the Antichrist from taking over – that he who must be taken out of the way – is the Body of Christ. The event that must happen is our gathering together unto Him. We are the salt of the earth and the light of the world. We preserve and hold the darkness back.

When we are gone, then will come the great falling away from all that is called God or that is worshipped. All the world will wonder after and worship the Antichrist. That will be the Great Tribulation, a time of judgment for the nation of Israel; a subject of prophecy.

While this is happening on earth, the Body of Christ stands before the Judgment Seat of Christ, which we have already covered. Jesus is coming for a Church without spot or wrinkle (Ephesians 5:27), to be his bride or wife. It is at the Judgment Seat that **"his wife hath made herself ready"** (Revelation 19:7). She is arrayed in fine linen, clean and white" (Revelation 19:8), **"for the marriage of the lamb is come"** (Revelation 19:7).

Check out the honeymoon: **"And I saw heaven opened, and behold a white horse; and he that sat upon him was called Faithful and True, and in righteousness he doth judge and make war. And the armies which were in heaven followed him upon white horses, clothed in fine linen, white and clean"** (Revelation 19:11, 14).

Our honeymoon is returning with Him to deliver the wrath to come in its final phase. Notice we were in heaven, not on earth. We have already been to the Judgment Seat of Christ and the Marriage of the Lamb. **"Behold, the Lord cometh with ten thousands of his saints, To execute judgment upon all"** (Jude 1:14-15a).

This is the time that the prophets and Christ prophesied about when Israel would be gathered from the four winds and brought into their promised land, along with all the tribulation saints.

This is your post-tribulation rapture. There is a post-tribulation rapture, it's just not for the Body of Christ. Notice that the tribulation saints **"keep the commandments of God, and the faith of Jesus"** (Revelation 14:12).

The Church is gone. It is no longer the Church Age. No more grace alone through faith alone. You have to have the faith of Jesus and keep the commandments of God, not take the Mark of the Beast (Revelation 20:4), and **"endure unto the end"** (Matthew 24:13). It's a totally different time and a totally different plan of salvation.

People will still get saved during the tribulation, but it'll probably cost them their heads. Thank God we live in the Age of Grace. We have a blessed hope, **"And the Lord direct your hearts into the love of God, and into the patient waiting for Christ"** (2 Thessalonians 3:5). **"For God hath not appointed us to wrath, but to obtain salvation by our Lord Jesus Christ"** (1 Thessalonians 5:9).

The blessed hope keeps your eyes on Jesus waiting for Him. Satan wants you to take that from you and get your eyes on yourself enduring unto the end, politics, the world around you, et cetera. Everything that the Devil slips in is designed to do just that – take your eyes off Jesus and put them back on you and this world.

So don't get confused. That is our blessed hope. When you rightly divide the Book and understand what is being spoken to whom, it all becomes crystal clear.

Chapter Ten – The Attack on Grace

Christ is become of no effect unto you, whosoever of you are justified by the law; ye are fallen from grace

Galatians 5:4

Satan is always trying to slip something in. There's nothing new. Much of Paul's ministry was defending the faith from those who were trying to add elements of Old Testament religion to the newly revealed gospel of grace. The whole book of Galatians was written to defend the truth of grace from this attack. Paul opens the epistle like this, **"I marvel that ye are so soon removed from him that called you into the grace of Christ unto another gospel: Which is not another; but there be some that trouble you, and would pervert the gospel of Christ"** (Galatians 1:6-7).

There are entire cultic religious groups based on this error, as well as elements of it in major Christian denominations. As always, the sword of the spirit will rightly divide this issue.

Everything in the Bible is *for* us, but everything in the Bible was not written *to* us. Paul puts it like this, **"For whatsoever things were written aforetime were written for our learning, that we through patience and comfort of the scriptures might have hope"** (Romans 15:4).

We learn from all scripture, but we are not to try and obey everything that God told every person in the Bible to do. There is no longer a literal tree in a garden that you may not eat of. God does not expect you to be building a big boat and rounding up livestock. You do not sacrifice animals for your sins. Those instructions were not for you. They were for somebody else in the past under a different covenant.

It is not the purpose of this chapter to expound on covenants and dispensations. That is another study. Satan is trying to bring the Christian back under the Old Testament covenant of the law.

As with everything he tries to slip in, this is designed to take your eyes off Christ and His finished work and to bring your focus back on yourself. Our question is this: What application has the law of Moses to the born again believer in the body of Christ? Let's define our terminology.

By "Christian," we mean a believer who has been born again by the Spirit of God and placed in the Body of Christ as covered in chapter 4.

What is the "law of Moses?" Eerdmans Bible's dictionary says, "Torah, the divine law or instruction according to which Israel was to live as stipulated in the covenant. Pentateuch, the first five books of the Old Testament that the Hebrew scriptures refer to as Torah. This designation appears in the Old Testament in such phrases as the law of Moses, the book of the law of Moses, the book of the law, and the book of the law of the Lord."

Simply, it is everything that Moses received from the Lord for the nation of Israel concerning the covenant of the law. It is a single unit but with layers like an onion. The heart of the law is the Ten Commandments.

Layered around them are layered all the other laws and regulations that flow out from the Ten. Around that is a layer of curses and punishments that result from breaking these laws. The next layer is the sacrificial system put in place to hold back God's judgment where there is faith and obedience.

This included the tabernacle, priests, sacrifices, feast days, seasons, and sabbaths. Obedience to the law brought physical, material blessing. This is the covenant given to the nation of Israel to govern them in the land God had given them.

After the resurrection of Christ and the coming of the Holy Spirit, the early Jewish believers continued to practice their religion as they and their ancestors had since they received it. The nation as a whole and the rulers and leaders continued to reject Christ. God closed the book on them and sent the gospel to the Gentiles.

That's everybody else. As the Gentiles began to get saved and form churches, many Jewish believers thought that the Gentiles should also follow the law of Moses. This issue came to a head and was settled once and for all at the council in Jerusalem in Acts chapter 15.

The problem? **"But there rose up certain of the sect of the Pharisees which believed, saying, That it was needful to circumcise them, and to command them to keep the law of Moses"** (Acts 15:5).

The verdict? **"And they wrote letters by them after this manner; The apostles and elders and brethren send greeting unto the brethren which are of the Gentiles in Antioch and Syria and Cilicia. Forasmuch as we have heard, that certain which went out from us have troubled you with words, subverting your souls, saying, Ye must be circumcised, and keep the law: to whom we gave no such commandment"** (Acts 15:23-24).

That should have been the end of it, but these Pharisees never gave up trying to drag the Gentile Christians back under Jewish religion. The term "Judaizers" has come to represent the situation addressed by Paul's letter to the Galatians.

These Judaizers wanted the Gentiles to be circumcised and obey all of the law of Moses including dietary laws, sabbaths, feast days, new moons, sabbatical years, etc. In Paul's view, this amounted to the substitution of a different gospel for the true gospel which would make the preaching and hearing of the gospel vain and would be a retreat from the spirit back to the flesh. Paul told the Romans, **"For Christ is the end of the law for righteousness to every one that believeth"** (Romans 10:4).

In 2 Corinthians chapter 3, Paul says that we are **"ministers of the new testament; not of the letter, but of the spirit"** (verse 6). He says that **"the ministration of death, written and engraven in stones . . . was to be done away"** (verse 7). He calls the law, **"that which is abolished"** (2 Corinthians 3:13). To the Colossians, Paul says, **"Blotting out the handwriting of ordinances that was against us, which was contrary to us, and took it out of the way, nailing it to his cross"** (Colossians 2:14).

The law of Moses had served its purpose. That inferior covenant has been done away with, abolished, and nailed to the cross. The veil of the temple had been torn wide open.

We all have free access to God in Christ without any element of the law. **"Wherefore the law was our schoolmaster to bring us unto Christ, that we might be justified by faith. But after that faith is come, we are no longer under a schoolmaster"** (Galatians 3 24:25).

Paul tells Timothy who the law is for now. It is **"not made for a righteous man, but for the lawless and disobedient, for the ungodly and for sinners"** (1 Timothy 1:9). Why is that? **"[F]or by the law is the knowledge of sin"** (Romans 3:20) and **"For as many as are under the works of the law are under the curse"** (Galatians 3:10).

Paul pleads with the Galatians, **"how turn ye again to the weak and beggarly elements, whereunto ye desire again to be in bondage? Ye observe days, and months, and times, and years. I am afraid of you, lest I have bestowed upon you labour in vain"** (Galatians 4:9-11). **"Are ye so foolish? having begun in the Spirit, are ye now made perfect by the flesh?"** (Galatians 3:3).

Paul says that we are either walking in the spirit or the flesh. He allows for no mixture of the two, for **"a little leaven leaveneth the whole lump"** (Galatians 5:9). Check out the context of that verse.

Jewish religion is exactly the leaven he was talking about. When we talk about this subject, someone will ask the question, "don't we become spiritual Jews in Christ? And doesn't that make everything for Israel for us too?"

This is what they're talking about: We as Gentile believers in the body of Christ have been grafted into God's channel of blessing in the seed of Abraham.

Paul describes this in Romans 11:17, **"And if some of the branches be broken off, and thou, being a wild olive tree, wert grafted in among them, and with them partakest of the root and fatness of the olive tree."**

It all started with Abraham. **"And he received the sign of circumcision, a seal of the righteousness of the faith which he had yet being uncircumcised: that he might be the father of all them that believe, though they be not circumcised; that righteousness might be imputed unto them also"** (Romans 4:11).

Paul expounds on this in Galatians 3:13-14, **"Christ hath redeemed us from the curse of the law, being made a curse for us: for it is written, Cursed is every one that hangeth on a tree: That the blessing of Abraham might come on the Gentiles through Jesus Christ; that we might receive the promise of the Spirit through faith."**

Now we come to the very point or time of our grafting into Abraham and his seed where the promise is made. **"He saith not, And to seeds [plural], as of many; but as of one, And to thy seed, which is Christ"** (Galatians 3:16).

When we are born again, the Holy Spirit places us in Christ and we receive the promise of the Spirit through faith and become a spiritual child of Abraham. In that sense, we become a spiritual Jew and belong to spiritual Israel. We become partakers of the spiritual element of the Abrahamic covenant in Christ, not part of the covenant of law through Moses.

Look at the next verse (17). **"And this I say, that the covenant, that was confirmed before of God in Christ, the law, which was four hundred and thirty years after, cannot disannul, that it should make the promise of none effect."**

Did you catch that? We are grafted into the spiritual covenant of faith through Abraham in Christ. And the law, which came along 430 years later, has nothing to do with that and has nothing to do with us. The law was for the physical seed of Abraham – the nation of Israel.

"Wherefore then serveth the law? It was added because of transgressions, till the seed should come to whom the promise was made" (Galatians 3:19).

What did Paul just say there? He said that the law of Moses was a temporary covenant for the nation of Israel to hold the Abrahamic covenant in place for them until Christ came. That pretty much answers our question, doesn't it? We can learn and receive much from God's dealings with Israel in the scripture. But as born again Christians, under grace, we are in no way, shape, or form under any part of God's covenant of law to Israel. To go back to the other side of the cross, to an inferior covenant, no longer in effect, or any part of that covenant, is to pervert the gospel of grace.

Paul said that he considered all that stuff dumb. He tells the believers to **"Stand fast therefore in the liberty wherewith Christ hath made us free, and be not entangled again with the yoke of bondage"** (Galatians 5:1).

Religion takes our eyes off Christ and puts them back on self. It becomes all about, "look what I'm doing." It's just flesh.

Jesus plus anything equals nothing. Jesus plus nothing equals everything. We are already as blessed as it is possible for God to bless us in Jesus Christ. We are complete in Him (Colossians 2:10) when Christ is in you.

No religious rituals, no ceremonies, no observances, and no Sabbaths can add anything to that.

Chapter Eleven - Counterfeits

And for this cause God shall send them strong delusion, that they should believe a lie

2 Thessalonians 2:11

Another attack on biblical Christianity today is the modern Charismatic movement. The groups caught up in this error believe that miraculous signs and wonders performed by the Christ and the apostles in the four gospels and the book of Acts are still in effect today.

The book of Acts is a transitional book. It records the transition from Israel to the Church. The special apostolic signs and wonders were part of God's prophetic program for Israel.

As God stops dealing with them as a nation, the apostolic signs and wonders fade away. The main two sign gifts that are emphasized in most charismatic groups are miraculous healing and speaking in tongues. Those were special apostolic gifts and faded off the scene with the apostles.

They were a package deal, and all ceased for the same reasons, but I will focus on just one here, speaking in tongues. Let's see what the Bible says about tongues.

It has been rightly stated that a text without a context is a pretext. Webster's dictionary defines pretext as "a purpose stated or assumed to cloak the real intention or state of affairs." In other words, it's an excuse. The modern Charismatic doctrine of speaking in tongues is built on scripture taken out of context and misapplied.

So, if we want to know what the Bible says about tongues, we need to look at and understand a whole lot more than a few verses in Acts and 1 Corinthians. We need the context. Miles Coverdale, who completed his translation of the English Bible in 1535, is also famous for this quote, "It shall greatly help ye to understand scripture if thou mark not only what is spoken or written, but of whom and to whom, with what words, at what time, where, with what circumstances, considering what goeth before and what followeth after."

Another important rule for interpreting scripture is the Law of First Mention. This rule states that the first time a word appears in scripture, how that word is used, sets the tone, associations, and basic meaning of the word throughout the rest of scripture.

The first mention of tongues, or languages, in the Bible is in Genesis chapters 10 and 11, where they came into being. Up until then, everybody spoke the same language. At Babel, other tongues were introduced as a judgment of God for man's belief, unbelief, and disobedience. Tongues were a sign of judgment.

Now observe the tone, associations, and basic meaning of tongues throughout the Old Testament in God's dealing with the nation of Israel.

Look at what Moses said, **"The Lord shall bring a nation against thee from far, from the end of the earth, as swift as the eagle flieth; a nation whose tongue thou shalt not understand"** (Deuteronomy 28:49).

Look what King David says in Psalm 81:4-5, **"For this was a statute for Israel, and a law of the God of Jacob. This he ordained in Joseph for a testimony, when he went out through the land of Egypt: where I heard a language that I understood not."**

"When Israel went out of Egypt, the house of Jacob from a people of strange language" (Psalm 114:1).

Isaiah warned them, **"For with stammering lips and another tongue will he speak to this people"** (Isaiah 28:11). **"Thou shalt not see a fierce people, a people of a deeper speech . . . that thou canst not understand"** (Isaiah 33:19).

Along comes Jeremiah about a hundred years later, **"Lo, I will bring a nation upon you from far, O house of Israel, saith the Lord: it is a mighty nation, it is an ancient nation, a nation whose language thou knowest not, neither understandest what they say"** (Jeremiah 5:15).

A few years later, Ezekiel 3:5-6 says, **"For thou art not sent to a people of a strange speech and of an hard language, but to the house of Israel; Not to many people of a strange speech and of an hard language, whose words thou canst not understand. Surely, had I sent thee to them, they would have hearkened unto thee."**

Tone, association, and basic meaning. What? God's judgment at the hands of a foreign nation. If you were a Jew in the first century, the time of Christ and the apostles, you would know all this history and understood the context of the sign of tongues.

When Jesus tells the Jews, **"your house is left unto you desolate"** (Luke 13:35), **"And when ye shall see Jerusalem compassed with armies, then know that the desolation thereof is nigh"** (Luke 21:20), **"And they shall fall by the edge of the sword, and shall be led away captive into all nations: and Jerusalem shall be trodden down of the Gentiles, until the times of the Gentiles be fulfilled"** (Luke 21:24).

This puts context to what He then said after his resurrection shortly before that judgment came, **"And these signs shall follow them that believe; In my name shall they cast out devils; they shall speak with new tongues"** (Mark 16:17).

They would continue to warn Israel about his coming judgment by the sign of tongues. And that is exactly what the apostles did on the day of Pentecost. They stood up and preached a message of condemnation upon Israel because they had murdered Jesus.

Notice carefully what the message preached in Acts chapters 2 and 3 is. Peter preaches the fact of the crucifixion but does not base any offer of salvation upon it. Rather, here the cross condemns those that hear the message.

There is nothing in these early messages about the death on the cross paying for an individual's sins as later revealed. Peter accuses and warns **"ye men of Israel . . . Jesus of Nazareth . . . ye have taken, and by wicked hands have crucified and slain"** (Acts 2:22-23). **"Save yourselves from this untoward generation"** (verse 40).

"But ye denied the holy one and the just . . ." (Acts 3:14a) **"and killed the prince of life"** (verse 15a). **"And it shall come to pass, that every soul, which will not hear that prophet, shall be destroyed from among the people"** (Acts 3:23).

Peter was speaking with new tongues and preaching judgment, and Israel understood.

Three thousand repented that first day and thousands more in the following days. Tongues only happen three times in the book of Acts. In each case there were Jews present who didn't believe something and **"the Jews require a sign"** (1 Corinthians 1:22).

In Acts chapter 2, there were a bunch of Jews who didn't believe that Jesus was their Messiah. In Acts chapter 10, a bunch of Gentiles spoke with tongues because there were Jews present who didn't believe that God would save the Gentiles.

In Acts chapter 19, God allowed a bunch of Jewish disciples of John the Baptist to speak in tongues because they had not yet believed on Jesus Christ. Israel was being warned and given a second chance to receive Jesus Christ. What was the national response from the rulers of the people and the nation as a whole? The Jews in Jerusalem gave their response by stoning Stephen while he was preaching Jesus to them.

In Acts 7 the Jews in Asia rejected the gospel. In Acts chapter 13, **"Then Paul and Barnabas waxed bold, and said, It was necessary that the word of God should first have been spoken to you: but seeing ye put it from you, and judge yourselves unworthy of everlasting life, lo, we turn to the Gentiles"** (verse 46).

The Jews in Europe also rejected the gospel. In Acts 18:6, Paul tells them, **"when they opposed themselves, and blasphemed, he shook his raiment, and said unto them, Your blood be upon your own heads; I am clean; from henceforth I will go unto the Gentiles."**

Finally, the Jews in Rome representing all the world rejected the gospel. In Acts 28:28, Paul tells them, **"Be it known therefore unto you, that the salvation of God is sent unto the Gentiles, and that they will hear it."**

This is what Paul is talking about concerning Israel in Romans 11:11, **"through their fall salvation is come to the Gentiles."** This was the fall of Israel.

Now, put all that in historical context. The Jews' rejection of Christ at Rome took place about 62 AD. Israel had been being warned by the sign of tongues of the coming judgment since Peter's first message on the day of Pentecost.

They hardened their hearts, rejected the warning, and rejected Christ. Eight years later, Titus of Rome marched his legions down and destroyed Jerusalem; just as prophecy and the sign of tongues had been warning. Israel would not be a nation again for almost 2,000 years.

The event that the sign of tongues had been warning about took place. God is done dealing with Israel as a nation until the end of the Church Age when they shall be restored. The book of 1st Corinthians is the only place that speaking in tongues is mentioned in the New Testament outside of the three times we talked about in the book of Acts.

The book of 1st Corinthians was written about 57 AD. This is 13 years before the destruction of Jerusalem. The sign of tongues was still in operation at that time and the church at Corinth was a very Jewish church. When Paul gets to Corinth around 54 AD, he lives and works with **"a certain Jew named Aquila"** (Acts 18:2-3), **"And he reasoned in the synagogue every sabbath, and persuaded the Jews and the Greeks"** (Acts 18:4).

"And he departed thence, and entered into a certain man's house, named Justus, one that worshipped God, whose house joined hard to the synagogue. And Crispus, the chief ruler of the synagogue, believed on the Lord with all his house" (Acts 18:7-8a).

Paul opens up his letters to Corinth with, **"For the Jews require a sign"** (1 Corinthians 1:22). When Paul gets to the chapter where he gives the rules for speaking in tongues, he reminds the Corinthians what tongues are for: **"In the law it is written, With men of other tongues and other lips will I speak unto this people; and yet for all that will they not hear me, saith the Lord. Wherefore tongues are for a sign, not to them that believe, but to them that believe not: but prophesying serveth not for them that believe not, but for them which believe"** (1 Corinthians 14:21-22).

That is so clear. What did he say? Tongues were for Israel. They were a warning that Israel would ignore. They were not for believers in Israel, but for unbelieving Jews, just as we have saw demonstrated through the whole Bible all the way back to Genesis. The whole chapter in 1 Corinthians is a rebuke for the way the Corinthians were abusing the gift of tongues in their church. The context of the whole chapter is in the local church.

Just to make sure everybody got that, Paul repeats the phrase seven times in the first chapter – verses 4, 5, 12, 19, 28, 34, and 35. There is nothing in 1 Corinthians or anywhere in the Bible about a spiritual prayer language that somebody's supposed to practice in private.

In order to create that teaching, you have to pull a couple verses out of their context and stick them together with bubble gum. It is make-believe. When Paul says**, "though I speak with the tongues of men and angels"** in 1 Corinthians 13:1, that is called "hyperbole."

Webster's defines it as "an extravagant exaggeration used as a figure of speech." Like saying, though I could leap tall buildings with a single bound, look at the multiple examples of exaggeration in this passage: Understand all mysteries. Have all faith. Remove mountains. Have all knowledge. Give my body to be burned. The first three verses of the chapter are hyperbole. Paul is not claiming these things. He is just saying, "even if." You can't create a spiritual prayer language out of that.

Another verse that is misunderstood to create this imaginary language is, **"Likewise the Spirit also helpeth our infirmities: for we know not what we should pray for as we ought: but the Spirit itself maketh intercession for us with groanings which cannot be uttered"** (Romans 8:26). Webster's dictionary defines "uttered" as "to send forth as a sound."

What you have in this verse is the Holy Spirit praying inside of you with groanings which are not sent forth as a sound. No sound, no words, no imaginary language.

Here's another one: **"For he that speaketh in an unknown tongue speaketh not unto men, but unto God: for no man understandeth him; howbeit in the spirit he speaketh mysteries"** (1 Corinthians 14:2).

Remember the context of the chapter. It is conduct in the church service. What Paul is telling them, that if there is no interpretation of what is said, then God is the only one who knows. Paul says much the same thing in verse 9, **"So likewise ye, except ye utter by the tongue words easy to be understood, how shall it be known what is spoken? for ye shall speak into the air."**

This all had to do with his rebuke of the church for speaking in tongues without an interpreter. **"But if there be no interpreter, let him keep silence in the church"** (1 Corinthians 14:28). There is no imaginary spiritual prayer language anywhere in these verses.

One more. **"He that speaketh in an unknown tongue edifieth himself; but he that prophesieth edifieth the church"** (1 Corinthians 14:4). It is not the act of speaking in tongues that edifies anyone. It is the content of the message when interpreted.

"Now, brethren, if I come unto you speaking with tongues, what shall I profit you, except I shall speak to you either by revelation, or by knowledge, or by prophesying, or by doctrine?" (1 Corinthians 14:6).

That is why Paul then says this, **"Wherefore let him that speaketh in an unknown tongue pray that he may interpret. For if I pray in an unknown tongue, my spirit prayeth, but my understanding is unfruitful"** (1 Corinthians 14:13-14).

If nobody knows what is being said, it is unfruitful and edifies no one. That's why the person doing the speaking must pray that he may interpret. Again, this is all about speaking in tongues and interpreting in the church service.

There is no imaginary prayer language anywhere in the chapter. In verse 15, Paul says that if he **"pray with the spirit,"** he will give **"the understanding also."** He says that if he **"sing[s] with the spirit,"** he will do the same in the church.

Everywhere tongues appear in scripture, they are known languages and can be interpreted. They are identified as soon as they show up. Luke first mentioned, **"every man heard them speak in his own language . . . And how hear we every man in our own tongue, wherein we were born?"** (Acts 2:6c, 8).

Paul said, **"There are, it may be, so many kinds of voices in the world, and none of them is without signification"** (1 Corinthians 14:10).

Webster's dictionary defines "signification" as "the meaning that a term, symbol, or character regularly conveys." In other words, not nonsensical babbling. Tongues as practiced today is unscriptural, deceptive, and worthless as a sign.

We need to judge our experiences and feelings by the word of God, not the other way around. Jeremiah 17:9 says, **"The heart is deceitful above all things, and desperately wicked: who can know it?"**

There's a lot of stuff that comes from our soul which can feel spiritual but is not. It is just emotion, self, and flesh. We cannot go by our feelings; we have to go by the Book. **"For the word of God is quick, and powerful, and sharper than any twoedged sword, piercing even to the dividing asunder of soul and spirit"** (Hebrews 4:12).

That sword will make a clean cut as we have just demonstrated, showing you what is from the Holy Spirit and what is not.

Paul was very clear, **"whether there be tongues, they shall cease"** (1 Corinthians 13:8). They were a warning sign to Israel. When Israel rejected the warning and Christ, they were cut off and tongues ceased, period. The same with the other sign gifts, including miraculous healing.

God still heals miraculously. He's God. He can do anything. We can all pray for healing for ourselves and for others. God will answer our prayers according to His will. The apostolic gifts were given to a person in the time of Christ and the apostles as signs fulfilling Old Testament prophecy to Israel. It was 100% effective **"and they were healed every one"** (Acts 5:16).

If healing existed today, that person should be going up and down the hallways of every children's hospital they could get to all day, every day, but no. Faith healers are crooks and fakes fleecing the flock. Their charismatic error places your focus on self, emotion, and counterfeit spiritual experiences.

The person under the spell of all that will not be walking in the real Holy Spirit and won't be able to **"rightly divid[e] the word of truth"** (2 Timothy 2:15). They will have to agree at some level to believe in make-believe, something that is either not real or not of God. Jesus is real, the Bible is real, the Holy Spirit is real, but when you attach things that are not real to them, you taint their credibility and cause people to throw the baby out with the bathwater.

Satan will point out all the fake stuff and say, "see, all that Jesus Bible stuff is phony." So, you see, what people always say, "as long as they preach Jesus, don't speak against what they're doing." No. Adding all that make-believe stuff to the gospel discredits the truth and purity of the message.

Let me give you a personal example or two. My mother was raised strict Roman Catholic. Not all the teachings of that church are wrong. They believe in the Father, Son, and the Holy Ghost. They believe in the death, burial, and resurrection of the Lord Jesus Christ. That's all good, but when you get to the part where sprinkling on a baby's head gets it into heaven, or a priest can forgive your sins, or a piece of bread turns into Jesus Christ and you receive Him in your mouth for salvation, that is all make-believe.

None of that is real, and my mom had enough sense to see that, and as soon as she was old enough, she got as far away from that as she could and never set foot in church again as long as she lived, except for weddings, funerals, and such. She threw the baby out with the bathwater. Because of the make-believe stuff attached to the truth, she rejected the truth all her life.

Satan is doing the same thing with the modern charismatic movement today. People see all that signs and wonders stuff for what it is and judge the whole of the Christian message in light of the make-believe.

We had a church group as guest speakers in our prison chapel. The speaker had men line up with medical problems. He was speaking nonsensical babbling at them, trying to command their legs to straighten out. The whole act.

I stepped out into the hallway and was watching through the window. Behind our chapel is the land where the pagan religions do their thing; Vikings, witches, Satanists, etc.

The prisoner in charge of that area, who is part of one of those groups, was also watching from the hallway. He looked over at me and he said, "Roy, I don't believe in that stuff, do you?" Think about that. An unsaved pagan convict had enough common sense to spot a con job when he saw it, while some of the brothers in our church, where I was serving as pastor, were lining up for this nonsense.

This is why those brothers are used to hearing truth from behind the pulpit. They trust the words of the men behind the pulpit. That is why it is the best place for the devil to slip something in.

Christians believe what their preachers tell them. That is why James 3:1 says, **"My brethren, be not many masters, knowing that we shall receive the greater condemnation."**

Preaching and teaching God's word is an awesome responsibility, and we shall be held accountable for every idle word spoken.

How can so many sincere Christians be so wrong about this subject of signs and wonders? Because they trusted the men who taught them, who trusted the men who taught him, who trusted a man who let the devil slip something in. It is not an innocent, harmless error. There is no such thing.

Dr. John R. Rice said, "you can't teach bad doctrine without doing harm." Trace error back to the spiritual realm. If a teaching is not true and scriptural, it did not come from the Holy Spirit. If it did not come from the Holy Spirit, where did it come from? There is only one other source. It is a **"doctrine of devils"** (1 Timothy 4:1), which is causing people to misrepresent and replace the actual work of the Holy Spirit before the church and the world.

"A little leaven leaveneth the whole lump" (Galatians 5:9). Paul was talking about Jewish religion in that verse, but the principle applies.

We have to keep it real. What we believe matters. What we believe affects what we do. What we do matters. If the devil can get you to believe wrong, he can get you to do wrong.

Section 3: Prologue

The Final Word

If you've made it to the end of this book, you may say at this point, "all you talked about was the Bible." Yep! Now you're getting it. The spiritual realm is just as real as the material world.

There are only two voices coming from that spiritual realm. There's the voice of Satan manifested through the spirits of the air and this world that they control. The other voice is the voice of God, and the Holy Spirit manifested in His word, the Holy Bible.

In the light of that truth and everything else we've covered in this book, listen one more time to Dr. Donald Gray Barnhouse, "Our whole world is an illusion created by Satan to deceive us and the only spiritual truth in life is to be found in the word of God. Those who refuse the word are unable to see because they have rejected light, have adopted other standards which they think are light and are therefore in greater darkness."

That just about sums it up. That is a hard truth. In the movie, *A Few Good Men*, Tom Cruise had Jack Nicholson in court on the witness stand and he tells Jack something like, "I want the truth," and Jack answers, "the truth, the truth, you don't want the truth, you can't handle the truth!"

That is true of most people. If there is something about Dr. Barnhouse's statement that offends you, that is a measure of where you are spiritually. A better quote for you might be one from Billy Sunday.

Brother Billy said, "the reason you don't like the Bible, you old sinner, is because it knows all about you."

Remember what Jesus said, **"He that is of God heareth God's words: ye therefore hear them not, because ye are not of God"** (John 8:47).

That was true when those words were spoken and just as true today, but so is this, **"But as many as received him, to them gave he power to become the sons of God, even to them that believe on his name: Which were born, not of blood, nor of the will of the flesh, nor of the will of man, but of God"** (John 1:12-13).

"Being born again, not of corruptible seed, but of incorruptible, by the word of God, which liveth and abideth for ever" (1 Peter 1:23).

"Marvel not that I said unto thee, Ye must be born again" (John 3:7).

God has just done an amazing, an amazing work. And my life's verse is Philippians 1:6, **"Being confident of this very thing, that he which hath begun a good work in you will perform it until the day of Jesus Christ."** And He will, and He is, and He does.

And so, no matter where you are in your life and your walk with God, it's never over. It's never too late. And there's nobody that He can't use if you just surrender your heart to Him. So, hey, give it all to Him. All of it.

Make Him that for real, for real, a hundred percent the head of your life and watch what God do. There are only three places that you can be, heaven, hell, or right here on earth.

So, while you're right here on earth, you have a decision to make about where you will go when you die, because you can't stay here. You can't go. You'll be checking out one day, and you're going up or you're going down.

Because heaven is a perfect place, right? God is a perfect and a holy God. And guess what? We ain't. We got sin. Amen. God can't let sin into his heaven, or it wouldn't be heaven.

Look at it this way. You got a mom who has that beautiful living room. I mean, with the white shag carpet and the velvet couches. I mean, that's that living room.

That's just for show. Nobody's even allowed to sit in it. That's a perfect, beautiful house, right? But she has all those kids, and they are out in the backyard playing in the mud. They're all dirty and it's time for dinner.

And mama comes out on the back porch, and she says, "Come on boys!" And they come up running up to the house and she's like, "Whoa, whoa, whoa, whoa, whoa! You're all covered with mud. You can't come in here like that!"

What does mama do? Well, there's a garden hose right there next to the door. And mama gets those kids, and she washes them off.

And I'm here to tell you that there's a fountain filled with blood. It's drawn from Emmanuel's veins and sinners plunged beneath that flood lose all their guilty stains. You see, Jesus Christ is the only way to heaven. Jesus Christ is the only way to get rid of your sins.

See, He went to the cross of Calvary and in a moment of time, all the sin of every man, woman, boy, and girl that was ever created in the universe was placed on the lovely Lord Jesus. And it was judged on Him. He did your time.

He paid your bail. He closed your account on Calvary. The death, burial, and the resurrection of the Lord Jesus Christ – this is the gospel.

It's not religion. There's nothing you can do to earn it. You could never be good enough. There's nothing you could do to keep it if you did earn it. Salvation is by grace through faith in the finished work of the Lord Jesus Christ. The Bible says that **"if thou shalt confess with thy mouth the Lord Jesus, and shalt believe in**

thine heart that God hath raised him from the dead, thou shalt be saved. For with the heart man believeth unto righteousness; and with the mouth confession is made unto salvation" (Romans 10:9-10).

And it's so simple. It's so simple.

Everyone wants to complicate it. When the Philippian jailer fell at the feet of the Apostle Paul in Acts 16:20-31, he said, **"what must I do to be saved?"** They said, **"believe on the Lord Jesus Christ and thou shalt be saved."**

He didn't say eat a biscuit. He didn't say, "go get dunked in some water." He didn't say, "join a church." He said, **"believe on the Lord Jesus Christ."**

When you accept that payment that He made for you on Calvary's cross, that blood is applied to you. It's a heart transaction. When you believe, you trust, you receive, and you accept the Lord Jesus, your heart opens. Then Jesus Christ and the person of his Holy Spirit comes inside of you and takes up residence. And your spirit is what? Born again.

That's what Jesus told Nicodemus in John 3:7. **"Ye must be born again."** How are we born again? By believing, accepting, and trusting the Lord Jesus Christ in our hearts.

That's all you can do. You can't earn it. You can't join a religion. You can't turn over a new leaf. You can't be good enough, but it's a free gift.

And all you must do is receive that gift. God said that He will come in and dwell with you and your heart. He that's joined with the Lord is one spirit. And you'll be seated in heavenly places in Christ Jesus. You will go to heaven when you die, or He comes to get you. That's salvation.

Pure and simple.

And that's the end of my book. Thank you for bearing with me. Love you. Now we'll serve you up some fresh bread, huh? Make some new videos. Amen.

God bless you.

About the Author

Brother Roy Bell (B.S., Th.M., Th.D.) is a missionary evangelist who was the pastor of the Christian church at Nevada's largest prison during his years of incarceration and now brings his no nonsense style of plain preaching to a wider congregation. Brother Roy's message is simple: Jesus is real and The Bible is true, period. "Believe on the Lord Jesus Christ, and thou shalt be saved . . ." (Acts 16:31).

Made in the USA
Coppell, TX
03 December 2024